psychic
intelligence

psychic
intelligence

TUNE IN AND DISCOVER THE POWER OF YOUR INTUITION

TERRY AND LINDA JAMISON,
THE PSYCHIC TWINS

GRAND CENTRAL
Life & Style
NEW YORK · BOSTON

Copyright © 2011 by Chrysalis Project, Inc.

Grand Central Life & Style
Hachette Book Group
237 Park Avenue
New York, NY 10017
www.HachetteBookGroup.com

Grand Central Life & Style is an imprint of Grand Central Publishing.
The Grand Central Life & Style name and logo are trademarks of Hachette Book Group, Inc.

The publisher is not responsible for websites (or their content) that are not owned by the publisher.

Printed in the United States of America

First Edition: June 2011

10 9 8 7 6 5 4 3 2 1

Library of Congress Cataloging-in-Publication Data
Jamison, Terry.
    Psychic intelligence: tune in and discover the power of your intuition / Terry and Linda Jamison.—1st ed.
        p. cm.
    ISBN 978-0-446-56342-0
    1. Psychic ability.   I. Jamison, Linda.   II. Title.
    BF1031.J24 2011
    133.8—dc22
                                                                    2010046546

For The Realm of One (our angelic soul family),
and all of our magical helpers, both visible and invisible.
You know who you are.

Acknowledgments

And when you want something, all the universe conspires in helping you to achieve it.

—Paulo Coelho, *The Alchemist*

For the longest time, this book seemed like the impossible dream. We are profoundly grateful to all the people who helped make it possible.

We would like to thank our father, Philip, and our mother, Jane, whom we sadly lost in 2008. Our parents taught us a great appreciation for art, humor, and creativity. Thanks also to our brother, Philip. Warm thanks go to our literary agent, Eileen Cope, at Trident Media Group, who enthusiastically embraced our project and shepherded it to the proper publisher, as well as to our great editor, Diana Baroni, and the entire team at Hachette. Thanks go out to our dear friends Robert Hernandez, Lisa Johnson Mandell, and Josette Prevost, who have long been our terrific support system behind the scenes. We appreciate the help of Natalie Kaire, who believed in us early on. We are very grateful to Judy Kern for her expert editorial guidance.

Special thanks should go to our web designer, Paul Hernandez, for his loyal support and friendship over the past four years. Thanks also to our friends Stephanie Liss and Ann Burckle; our publicist, Sylvia Desrochers; and our wonderful attorney, Rick Brull. We wouldn't be walking around without the special healing talents of our chiropractor, Dr. Geraldine Greenberg, and our classical homeopath, Michalene Seiler.

We'd especially like to mention Daisaku Ikeda, our spiritual mentor, who taught us to strive to achieve what we thought we could not. Finally, we extend deep appreciation to all of our friends and clients here and abroad who have taught us so much about psychic intelligence, friendship, and love, and who have given us many invaluable gifts. This book is for you.

Contents

PART III

TOOLS FOR TUNING IN TO YOUR POWERS

PART IV

PUT YOUR POWERS TO WORK

Authors' Preface

The book you are holding in your hands has been a lifetime in the making. The road less traveled has been, for us, a long and winding path leading to many dimensions of ourselves. This road did not exist until we beat a trail through the jungle with machetes! Believe us when we tell you it wasn't easy, but it has been an exotic and rewarding trip. We have paved the road, and now we are ready to be your tour guides on what we hope will become a multidimensional superhighway.

We want our book to be the twin-essential guide to the paranormal. While it could have been as long as an encyclopedia, we wanted to keep it concise and digestible. Less is more. There is a lot of profound information to be had here. Therefore, we recommend reading it over a period of time, and not too quickly, so you can better process the knowledge incrementally, practice the exercises, and integrate them into your life.

When spiritual teacher Andrew Cohen was asked why people responded in an extreme way to his teachings, he replied, "Because I'm trying to create something *new*—something that has never happened before. And this provokes tremendous resistance. This is how evolution works—the old always resists the new. And the people who meet the most resistance are those who step out ahead in pursuit of a vision of that which has not yet emerged." We know all too well what this feels like. We have persevered in the face of impossible odds to create something new. But it has all been worth it, and this book is the result of our efforts and sacrifices.

We think that more and more people are developing the ability to see into alternate windows or dimensions of reality. We are at the vanguard of a powerful movement that will transform the way we as a culture view and influence reality. Won't you take this journey with us?

Buckle up! Ready for liftoff! You are about to enter The Psychic Twins Zone.

psychic intelligence

PART I

THE PSYCHIC IN ALL OF US

Most people associate intelligence with our ability to acquire knowledge on a conscious level. But psychic intelligence has more to do with a profound, subconscious knowing that transcends time and space. We are professional psychics, but every single one of you also has the ability to tap into this higher source of knowing and to use that information to create a better life for yourself. Why, then, isn't everyone using this innate gift to the best of their ability?

To begin this book, we'll explain why you may have lost touch with your own psychic intelligence and what you can do to get it back.

You've got it; all you need are the tools to recognize and cultivate it, and the courage and self-confidence to put it into action.

The Psychic Twins—Who We Are and What We Do

You may think that because we are identical twins and share the same DNA we're naturally more telepathic than most. And in fact, we do have twin telepathic experiences on a daily basis. We don't need BlackBerrys or iPhones to communicate with each other; we use "TwinBerry" mental telepathy.

But according to Guy Lyon Playfair, a researcher of the paranormal and author of *Twin Telepathy*, only about 30 percent of twins have actually experienced a telepathic connection while the vast majority have no particular psychic bond between them. We, however, were born not only with the ability to communicate psychically with each other, but also with abilities that reach beyond our twinship, which enable us to be reliably psychic for anyone at any time.

In West Chester, the small Pennsylvania farming town where we grew up, no one had ever heard of—much less met—a psychic, and so for a long time neither we nor our family and friends thought much about our abilities. Although both our parents were artists— our father, Philip Jamison, is a master watercolorist and national academician, and our mother was also a gifted painter—they were in many ways quite conservative. While they applauded our inherited artistic talents, they tended to either dismiss or discourage our ability to "know" things we had no way of knowing.

The first psychic experience either one of us can recall occurred when we were five and Terry won a prize at her school fair for correctly naming the exact number of jellybeans in a jar. She didn't just guess the closest number—she was *exactly right*. Later, as teenagers, we started predicting what our friends' careers would be—although we didn't learn until many years after that our predictions had come true. Still, we always had the sense that we would become famous artists and designers, and we didn't spend a lot of time thinking about how or why we seemed to know or predict things other people simply could not foresee.

It wasn't until our mid-teens, when we started to experience a series of baffling and debilitating health issues, that we began our continuing quest for spiritual knowledge. It was that ongoing search that eventually led us to discover the Buddhist philosophy and practice that provided us with spiritual sustenance during those years of physical pain, as it continues to do today.

All our lives, we believed there was a philosophy that could help us find answers. We had already tried many different meditation techniques and spiritual practices when our friend Susan invited us to attend a Buddhist meeting. We found ourselves sitting on the floor of someone's small apartment, surrounded by people facing a scroll in a box on the wall and chanting in a language we didn't understand. Their combined voices chanting in total harmony sounded very much like music. But it was the genuine excitement of the people sharing their personal experiences and the benefits they'd received from the practice that impressed us the most. These people had an irrepressible spirit, fueled by their faith that any obstacle could be overcome. Somehow we knew this was the practice that was going to help us. Since that first meeting, Buddhism has empowered us to discover new dimensions of courage, strength, and resilience we never knew we had.

Still, the path that eventually led to our current work has been neither straightforward nor easy. After graduating high school, we studied painting and sculpture at the Pennsylvania Academy of Fine Arts, and we received BFA degrees in painting and art education from Tyler School of Art, Temple University, in Philadelphia. Then, after college, we moved to New York City and began our careers as comedic performance artists. We started our own company called Pop Theatrics, and we entertained at events for luminaries such as Bob Hope, Luciano Pavarotti, Jacqueline Onassis, Donald Trump, and Cher, and at the White House for then-president Ronald Reagan and his wife. We even starred in a short film written especially for us that aired on *Saturday Night Live*. This was a huge honor and definitely one of the highlights of our theatrical career. Every comic dreams of being on *SNL*, and we got on the show without even auditioning!

After twelve years in New York, we moved to Los Angeles hoping to further our television and film careers as comic actresses. As we honed our stand-up act at the Improv and the Comedy Store in Hollywood, we were also, quietly and deliberately, developing our innate abilities as psychics and mediums. Although we'd been practicing tuning in to our intuition for some time, we became especially interested in psychic work in our twenties. Having spent years battling chronic illness and pain, we instinctively knew that the medications our doctors had been prescribing weren't helping us, and we believed we could use our psychic abilities to discover a more healing path.

To get the answers we needed, we began to work with a pendulum (a form of dowsing that's similar to using a Y-shaped stick or rod to find water or metal in the ground). We would hold the pendulum dangling from a string and ask questions with simple yes or no answers, such as whether a particular medicine or therapy would be positive for us, or whether we should take a particular job. Having decided that a yes answer would make the pendulum circle clockwise and a no answer would cause it to circle counterclockwise, we gave ourselves that autosuggestion. To give yourself an autosuggestion, you simply have a clear intention and state out loud the outcome you've decided upon—in this case that the pendulum's circling clockwise would indicate yes, and its circling counterclockwise would indicate no. Early on, we would even take the pendulum to the grocery store and ask it whether or not a particular food would be beneficial to our health. Many years ago, our friends were trying to talk us out of moving to Los Angeles, but when we asked the pendulum if we should move, the answer was a clear yes. California has now been our home for twenty years.

At the same time we were working with the pendulum to figure out how to improve our health, we also worked extensively with alternative therapies, including Chinese medicine, acupuncture, classical homeopathy, various forms of chiropractic, countless special diets, and different types of prayer and meditation. We even went to shamanic healers. In the end, we became our own best diagnosticians, and in the process discovered what would become an important aspect of our life's work, which is medical intuition. Our heightened awareness of illness made us especially sensitive to others' diseases and disorders, and we have been doing medical intuitive work for many years now. (For more on this, see Chapter Ten.)

We'd been making predictions for friends and using our psychic abilities for years without really thinking of them as anything special when, one day, we were sitting at a charming little place called The Rose Café in Venice Beach, California, and Linda began spontaneously writing on a napkin. The words seemed to come out of nowhere, and before she knew it she'd filled five napkins with writing. At the time, she really had no idea what was happening, but we later learned she had been in a state that's known as a "conscious trance" and doing channeled or automatic writing. When we returned home, Terry felt compelled to try automatic writing, too. She soon realized that she also had this gift, which ultimately became, and still remains, our primary tool for receiving psychic information about the past, present, and future. Interestingly, Terry's automatic handwriting looks quite different from Linda's. Linda's writing is loopy and embellished with elaborate flourishes and curlicues, very much like a medieval manuscript. Terry's writing is a smaller script, with flat lines and words sometimes joined together. It somewhat resembles an earthquake seismogram. Neither of these writing styles bears much resemblance to our normal writing.

Shortly after we moved to Los Angeles we figured out that there weren't many acting jobs calling for adult twins (unless your last name was Barbi and you worked with a stripper pole), but our psychic reputation was spreading by word of mouth, mostly through friends, and eventually we posted a tiny ad for our services in a small local publication. Much to our surprise, a producer for NBC television saw it and called us. After asking us to confirm that we were really twins and really psychics, she challenged us to do a spontaneous reading for her over the phone, which we did. She told us that we had just given her the most accurate reading she'd ever had, and invited us to appear with Sylvia Browne (who was, at the time, probably the best-known psychic in the country) and three other intuitives on an NBC program called *The Other Side*. It was the first of three appearances on that show, and we diagnosed people's illnesses on the air, with a respected doctor verifying our accuracy. The Psychic Twins were off and running!

Over the years we've appeared on more than one hundred television and radio programs and starred in fifteen documentary films profiling our psychic gifts. And we have made countless public predictions of world events—most notably the 9/11 attacks on the World Trade Center and the Pentagon on Art Bell's *Coast to Coast AM* radio program on November 2, 1999—that have cemented our reputation and made us the most documented psychics in the world. We've assisted law enforcement in solving murder cases, reunited families, predicted all kinds of natural disasters, and even diagnosed serious medical conditions and diseases.

But it's the work we do quietly and in private that has been our greatest reward. For more than twenty-five years now we have helped thousands of clients all over the world to gain insight into their past, better understand their present, and determine their true purpose.

Our role, as we see it, is to shine a light into the darkness of the unknown so that people are better able to trust their own intuition, understand the mysterious world in which we live, gain a new perspective that allows them to make better choices, and create a more authentic and meaningful life for themselves.

Rather than simply persuading or convincing others of our predictive "rightness," we seek to enroll and empower them to discover for themselves what is possible on a personal and spiritual level. Our intention is to be the bridge that allows people to feel more connected, not only with one another but also with the energy of the Universe. We know that what we do is serious business, and while we go about it with humor as well as compassion, we always take it very seriously. Being a good psychic medium requires courage, intelligence, integrity, and most important, *heart*.

For us, tapping into the psychic energy of the Universe is as natural as breathing. It's no more difficult than turning on the radio, tuning in, and receiving information. We know that's not always easy for most people to believe, much less achieve. But we also know that everyone has some innate level of intuitive ability, and our goal in this book is to help you discover and nurture your own (natural) supernatural talents. You, too, can access this higher level of understanding that will allow you to unleash your true unlimited potential.

In the following chapters we'll explain the factors that may have been preventing you from accessing your own psychic intelligence, how you can overcome those stumbling blocks, and what you can do to enhance the intuitive abilities you were born with. Not all psychics receive information the same way. As you'll be learning, some people are better at receiving psychic information in auditory form, others "see" mental images, some people are more emotionally sensory, and still others simply "know" what's coming to them from the spirit world. These four ways of getting in touch with your psychic intelligence are what we call "the four Clairs," and we'll be showing you how to determine where your particular psychic talents lie. Once you know that, you'll not only be able to tap into whatever turns out to be your primary source of wisdom, but you'll also be able to use the methods we'll provide to enhance those areas where you may be less innately intuitive.

We'll help you become more adept at peeking around corners to see both the warning signs and the positive signals the Universe is sending your way. We'll provide you with all the psychic tools you need to define your dreams and ambitions so that you can discover your true life purpose, enhance your love life, improve personal relationships, enjoy vibrant good health, and bring more wealth and abundance into your life.

A friend once told us, "You are two of the few people I know who are truly living an authentic life." It was a great compliment, and hard won. But we are here to tell you that if you just listen to that still, small voice within you and use the tools we provide, you, too, will find your wondrous authentic path and become the person you were meant to be.

2

Psychic Intelligence 101

M any people these days have lost touch with their own
intuitive abilities and are extremely skeptical of anyone's
ability to access any higher source of knowledge. As a culture, we
seem to be paranormally challenged. We have become so dependent
on modern technology and scientific proof that we no longer understand or appreciate the kind of spirit wisdom that was venerated by
our ancestors. We are so preoccupied with the material world that we
discount as superstition or fantasy the divine and subtle magical phenomena that were rich and natural parts of all ancient cultures.

What we now refer to casually—even dismissively—as "woman's
intuition" was once valued as a profound source of knowledge. But
according to the sociologist and cultural historian Riane Eisler, there
has been a global shift from spiritual, egalitarian, nonviolent goddess-
worshipping societies to patriarchal societies over the last six thousand
years. The ancient matriarchal societies, based on partnership and
creativity, were much more spiritually evolved than the technological societies of today. Over time, however, empathy, intuition, and a
connection with nature—values that were and still are associated with
women—were suppressed in favor of the logical, linear thinking associated with masculinity.

Whereas women were initially revered as intuitive healers, beginning in the late Middle Ages, Church-educated male "physicians" began to take over this traditionally female role. Channelers, healers, seers, and psychics of all kinds were labeled "witches" because of their ability to communicate with other realms, and, under Church auspices, millions of women were hunted down, tortured, and killed for practicing healing and intuitive arts.

Our intention is not to pit women against men, but to help you understand that there are two basic ways of acquiring knowledge. One is linear and logical; the other is spiritual and intuitive. True wisdom resides in the ability to appreciate and access the power of both. The two of us are often criticized and even ridiculed for what we do and for helping others to understand that these abilities exist. Nevertheless, we have proved it, and now we are sharing our secrets with you. To us, paranormal is the "new" normal!

Twintuition Tip:
Open your mind to expand your life.

Objection! Overruled!

In the fifteenth century, during the Inquisition, Nostradamus, who was predicting the future through pagan oracles, feared persecution and had to obscure his predictions by using anagrams, transposed letters, plays on words, and other cryptic methods in order to avoid imprisonment or being executed as a heretic. In a letter to his son, Cesar, he wrote, "I really did not want to write the documentations down concerning the future, mainly because of the insults I will earn.... The present form of governing parties will undergo tremendous changes in the future.... This is the reason why I mystified the real sense of my quatrains."

In the seventeenth century, Galileo, the father of modern astronomy, was considered a heretic and thrown into prison for suggesting that the sun rather than the earth was, in fact, at the center of the Universe. Skeptics and naysayers flatly refused to look through his telescope to see for themselves that he was right.

Today, many skeptics similarly refuse to look through our lens to see if there might be some truth to what we experience in the metaphysical world. They would rather reject even the possibility of an expanded reality than have to question and reevaluate their own long-held beliefs.

People often ask us why we don't respond to skeptics. Our answer is that no matter how many successful predictions we make, nothing is going to change their minds—and, therefore, cause them to admit they were wrong. Skeptics tend to reflexively condemn anything that strikes them as unorthodox or foreign. People tend to be afraid of what they don't understand, and we've found that the biggest skeptics are often those who feel threatened by their own intuitive potential, who shut down, and who then project their resentment onto us. They're resentful because they can't do what we do, which is silly and unfair. After all, they're the ones preventing themselves from becoming more intuitive. Or, to put it another way, we can't fix cars, but we're not resentful of car mechanics.

There was one time, however, when Linda found herself in the deep end of the jury pool (so to speak) and felt it necessary to respond. When she was called for jury duty a few years ago, she was impaneled on a criminal case, and when it was her turn to be questioned during the voir dire the judge asked her to describe her occupation. "I'm a professional clairvoyant and psychic detective," Linda answered, much to the judge's amusement. "Well, this is a first in my courtroom!" he exclaimed. "Do you have a psychic feeling about this trial's outcome?" And she said that indeed she did. The other jurors were giggling and the accused looked uncomfortable, but the attorneys were not amused. They began to cross-examine Linda as if *she* were the one on trial. The first lawyer to question her simply couldn't understand why she wouldn't be able to make a judgment based solely on the evidence presented in court. When Linda said she had a "sixth sense" that would make it difficult for her not to share her "gut feelings" with her fellow jurors during deliberation, he was really annoyed. The real kicker, however, came when a young female attorney, who obviously thought she was being very clever, smugly asked Linda to "predict" what her next question was going to be. There were audible gasps, but Linda, undaunted, proceeded to boldly predict exactly what the woman's next question would be. Obviously, she got it right because the red-haired lawyer's face turned bright crimson, and she stammered, "I have no more questions, Your Honor." Shortly thereafter Linda was dismissed. That experience just reinforced our long-held understanding that there are still many, many people who continue to doubt and get spooked by the validity of psychic intelligence.

It is almost shocking to see how stubbornly resistant people can be to acknowledging psychic abilities, even when the evidence is staring them in the face. But experiences such as Linda's have only served to galvanize our resolve and reinforce our steadfast intention to bring our work as teachers and intuitives into the world, even if it means encountering skeptics and naysayers who refuse to understand. These experiences simply show us how necessary our mission to educate people really is.

> For the truly faithful, no miracle is necessary. For
> those who doubt, no miracle is sufficient.
>
> —Nancy Gibbs

Five Psychic "Myth-Understandings"

We believe that much of the skepticism about psychics stems from the fact that there are so many misunderstandings and myths about what psychics do or should do. These are just a few that we've come up against over and over again:

*Myth #1: Psychics Were Not Mentioned in the Bible,
the Torah, or Buddhist Teachings, So Believing in Psychic
Phenomena Must Be Sacrilegious*

Contrary to popular belief, many world religions and traditions have stories of prophecies and seers.

The Old Testament contains many stories of major prophets, including Isaiah, Jeremiah, Ezekiel, and Daniel, along with those of literally scores of minor prophets. To take just a few examples, the Bible says that three wise men were guided by the North Star, on the advice of Isaiah, who also predicted the birth of the Messiah, which is a medieval term for "psychic." Numbers 11:25 states: "And the Lord came down in a cloud, and spake unto him [Moses], and took of the spirit that was upon him, and gave it unto the seventy elders: and it came to pass, that, when the spirit rested upon them, they prophesied, and did not cease." In Exodus 15:20 Miriam is referred to as a prophetess, as is Deborah in Judges 4:4. And 1 Chronicles 25:3 states that the sons of Jeduthun "prophesied with a harp, to give thanks and praise to the Lord."

In Buddhism the Buddha Nichiren predicted calamities in various sutras. For example, *The Sutra of Golden Light* (or *Sutra of Golden Splendor*) asserts that the four heavenly kings will abandon a nation whose rulers do not propagate the Dharma (the cosmic order or law). *The Great Collection Sutra* (or *Sutra of the Great Assembly*) predicts famine, war, epidemics, and other apocalyptic events if the ruler does not prevent the Dharma from perishing. And *The Benevolent Kings Sutra* predicts the departing of sages and the coming of seven calamities of a human, natural, and astronomical nature.

In modern times, the foundation of the Church of Jesus Christ of Latter-day Saints is based upon the prophecies of Joseph Smith, whom Mormons consider to be a modern prophet.

Myth #2: Psychics Should Know Everything

This is a surprisingly common misconception. Professional psychics are not omniscient, and should not claim to be! If we were omniscient, we would be God. And we would charge about a million dollars an hour. Along the same line, psychics can rarely predict the exact date and time when an event will occur. It is more realistic to expect a potential time frame. The future is fluid, and there is no absolute reality. The future is not written in stone. With our free will and intention, we can actually influence events, outcomes, and their timing. We can even change our destiny. In fact, the tools we give you in this book are designed to help you do just that.

Nevertheless, when we're appearing on live television, we are always held to the highest standards and expected to be perfect. TV producers and interviewers want us to spout astonishing revelations as if we were Nostradamus on a caffeine high. No pressure, right? Knowing that we can't control which spirit energies come through makes it that much harder to deliver what's expected of us on camera, when millions of viewers are judging us with a critical eye. We're sometimes tempted to ask the host whether he or she would expect a brain surgeon to perform neurosurgery on cue during a TV interview.

As psychics, we process all the information we receive through our human filters and past experiences, just as a portrait painter has his own personal style and way of interpreting his subject. We get what we get. For a lot of reasons, no one can predict every single major event that will happen in someone's life in sixty minutes or less.

In addition, some clients come for a reading with the tacit expectation that they will be assured of their future happiness, riches, fame, a gorgeous and caring soul mate, robust health and longevity, and—oh yes—a guest spot on *The Tonight Show.*

No psychic can guarantee your future, and if any psychic promises you that it will be perfect, you should probably ask for your money back. We can offer spiritual tools you can use to mitigate or circumvent a negative event or experience, but, as we've said, you have free will, and we can't follow you around like the medium portrayed by Whoopi Goldberg in the movie *Ghost* to make sure you are making the best and wisest choices for your life. While we do believe that we all come into this life with a soul blueprint—including who our parents will be, who our children will be, our careers, the major life lessons we'll learn—already mapped out, we also believe that there is no such thing as a fixed or absolute reality. The future is malleable, or, as it is put in Buddhism, "mutable."

Once a woman came to us and we gave her detailed guidance about her career, her relationships, her past lives, and what she might have coming up within the next few years. She seemed pleased and left with a spring in her step. The next day she called and said in a testy tone, "Why didn't you tell me that I was pregnant?" We had to laugh, because it made us feel that some people will never be satisfied with a reading no matter how much help you try to give them. They simply are not ready to accept the gift.

As spiritual counselors, we teach people—as we will be teaching you—how to maximize their individual potential and increase their chances of success. It is, however, totally unreasonable for people to expect a psychic to divine every detail of their past, present, and future lives.

Myth #3: Psychics Should Be Able to Predict Lotto Numbers

We once heard a famous talk show host say that she thought psychics were all frauds because if they were truly psychic, they would automatically win the lottery and, therefore, be extremely wealthy. Once again, psychics are not omniscient. Also, as we have often said, our gift is for other people: to help them live better lives, make wiser choices, and find their authentic path. It is not about becoming wealthy.

Myth #4: Mediums Are More Gifted Than Psychics

It is a myth that "mediums" (people who connect directly with the energies of specific individuals who have passed over) are somehow more gifted than "psychics" (people who have the ability to predict future events or describe past lifetimes, for example). This is like saying that singers are more gifted than dancers. In both cases, the information is coming from the world of spirit, even though the messengers and methods of delivery may differ.

In fact, some people have both abilities. We, for example, practice mediumship *and* predict future events. One is not necessarily a more advanced gift than the other. They both involve a certain level of skill and the ability to tap into higher dimensions or energy fields.

Myth #5: Psychics Shouldn't Charge for What They Do Because Their Ability Is a Spiritual Gift

This myth may stem from the old belief that money is "the root of all evil" and a truly spiritual person must give of him- or herself with no expectation of getting anything in exchange. Baloney! Intuitive counseling is a valuable service and no less worthy than any other form of counseling. A good psychic reading can be life-changing. Talented psychic readers deserve to be fairly compensated for their time, experience, and expertise. In addition, if there is no monetary investment, the client might not take the reading as seriously and could very well dismiss the guidance altogether.

How to Spot a Fake Psychic

Now that you know what a psychic should or should not be expected to do, you'll be better able to spot the genuine article and avoid being taken in by a fake. There isn't any licensing exam for psychics, and many people have been burned by con artists. Every field has its share of unscrupulous people who exploit others, and the psychic world is no different. But there are plenty of warning signs that should tip you off.

- A fake psychic may tell you that you have a curse, a dark cloud, or negative energy that he or she needs to clear with the use of rituals or the burning of special candles (at a hefty additional price!).
- A fake psychic has no track record of publicly documented accurate predictions (their own blog page doesn't count). Many claim to have predicted major world events but have no way to prove it. Don't let a flashy website fool you! Check the

practitioner's credentials, and if you have any doubts, try to get a good reference from someone you trust.

- Fakes often call themselves hokey names like "Spirit Warrior," "Psychic Sonia," "Madame Rose," "Aura Star," "Rainbow," "Light Goddess," and so forth. Use caution in believing their inflated claims.

- They may tell you that "you will come into a lot of money soon" or "there is money around you" but make no mention of how the money will manifest itself.

- Fake psychics often claim to be able to reunite you with a lost love. No one can do that but you! If he or she left, it may be a good thing!

- A fake psychic will often say he or she is "world-renowned" or "famous" without having any evidence or documented accomplishments to substantiate that claim.

- Fake psychics don't predict probable dates, times, or locations. They speak in vague generalities like "He's coming, I can see him...He's right around the corner...You won't be alone." Or "I see trains, planes, and bridges." A prediction that is so generalized it could apply to anyone, anywhere, at any time isn't really a prediction at all.

Use Your Inner Crystal Ball

There are so many charlatans in the business that it can be difficult to know whether or not a professed psychic or medium is ethical or sincere. But just because you may have had a bad experience with one person, we hope that you won't throw the baby out with the bathwater, as they say. Be willing to open your mind to the existence of legitimate psychic intelligence and give yourself the opportunity to experience and benefit from your own psychic gifts. If you believe that you might have intuitive abilities, you are opening the door; if you believe that you don't and will never have such gifts, you're making sure that you'll never find out!

Open Your Mind to the Wisdom of a Higher Intelligence

Interestingly, it's the modern science of quantum physics that has taught us energy never dies, it just keeps changing form, and everything, including our thoughts, has energy. What this means is that the energy of all the thoughts of all humankind still exists as a kind of universal consciousness that we can tap into for guidance. Since ancient times there have been various terms used to describe this universal source of knowledge that is outside of time and space, but it is a concept that has persisted throughout recorded history—from the *Unus mundus* to Carl Jung's collective unconscious to postmodern superstring theory. According to the writer and philosopher Terence McKenna, "The substance of the universe is consciousness, not matter." Our thoughts and the universal reality we live in can be compared to a kind of cosmic soup composed of an infinite number of invisible energy fields that contain infinite amounts of information. We humans are constantly downloading, decoding, and interpreting this information with our five senses in the same way that a computer downloads and decodes information from cyberspace.

As humans, we identify so strongly with our bodies and our finite, tangible world that we come to believe it is the only reality. Yet there are myriad realities and dimensions that we simply cannot perceive with our physical senses. Our higher intelligence vibrates at a higher frequency than our everyday thoughts and is what allows us to tap into this collective universal consciousness. We can all use our sixth sense to develop our brains and hearts so that we are able to access that universal consciousness and become dynamic filters for psychic intelligence.

> You are an infinite, limitless, immortal, universal and eternal
> energy temporarily residing in a body. You know that nothing
> dies, that everything is an energy that is constantly changing.
> —Wayne Dyer, *Manifest Your Destiny*

3

We Are All Psychic

Psychic, intuitive, paranormal—all these words describe aspects of what we generally think of as the supernatural. The dictionary defines "supernatural" as something above or beyond what is explainable by natural laws or phenomena; exceeding normal or expected capability. Most people associate it with something miraculous or transcendent; a mythical, godlike, or ghostly being, or a fictional superhero who has "superpowers" beyond the capability of us mere mortals.

In truth, however, we all have that inner superhero waiting to be discovered.

We all have the ability to tap into the source of higher intelligence that lies within each of us in order to become happier, healthier, and more fulfilled in every aspect of our lives. The job of each and every one of us, our life's work if you will, is to find the place within that leads us to create the life we were meant to live.

Has anyone ever asked you, "How did you know that?" or said, "Wow, you must be psychic!" Or maybe you have wondered yourself how you just "knew" something, or had a gut feeling about a person or an upcoming event. Everyone does from time to time. But most people just shake their heads and write it off as a coincidence or come up with some logical explanation for that which, in fact, defies logic. No one ever seems to question having a sense of humor or a sense of direction, a business sense or a fashion sense, but just mention having a sixth sense and people will look at you funny. In truth, however, your sixth sense is nothing more than your intuition, which is operating—mostly without your being aware of it—all the time.

Some people are naturally gifted athletes or musicians or visual artists, just as some people are more naturally gifted psychics. But we all have intuitive abilities that can be honed and developed like any other talent or gift. Think of it this way: We don't all have perfect pitch or the talent to become a world-renowned concert pianist, but if we practice, we can all learn to play basic melodies on the piano. And the same is true for developing whatever psychic skills we've been given.

Children Are Naturally Psychic

One key to developing any kind of gift or talent is simply believing that you can do it. Children are born with this kind of belief in their own omnipotence. Kids have no inner filter telling them what is or isn't possible, and they believe that whatever they imagine can become reality. As children we all sense that we have the power to make anything happen. It isn't until the adults in our world convince us our powers aren't real that we begin to doubt ourselves.

Kids believe in angels, Santa Claus, the tooth fairy, and the Easter bunny. Many children have invisible friends with whom they communicate as freely as we talk to our flesh-and-blood friends. We have a client named Geri, who, when she was six or seven, had an imaginary friend she called "Linka." Geri was quite sickly as a child, and Linka would come to her as a comforting and calming presence when she lay in bed. She would often hear Linka calling her name, and her sister said that Geri would literally turn and talk to her friend. Our point is that these are *not* imaginary friends. They are real spirits communicating from another dimension, and Geri was obviously clairvoyant and clairaudient.

Some children, of course, are more intuitive than others. They are born with a psychic gift, just as some are born with a beautiful singing voice or great hand-eye coordination. These highly intuitive children can experience dreams that come true or sense when someone is going to die or have an accident. They can look into someone's eyes and know who he or she has been in a past life, or whether that person is lying to them. Some young people have written to us about seeing shadowy figures at night or seeing glowing balls of light that

PSYCHIC IN UTERO

We received this amazing account from Kevin:

In January 1998 my wife, Stanna, began the third trimester of her pregnancy, and she started to notice when our unborn son would suddenly tumble wildly in her womb. For a week she wrote down the times, and then she told me about it.

As I looked at her list of times, they seemed oddly familiar to me. They were the times I clocked out of work. She continued to note the times of unborn Ryan's boisterous tumbling, and they continued to match the time I was heading home from work. As February began, however, I started meeting tax clients at their homes after work and Ryan's tumbling times changed to when I was leaving the client— not the time I called to say I was on my way, but the actual time I started the car.

The [fetal] tumbling was so reliable that when Stanna was visiting a friend who didn't have a phone and she knew where my client lived, she'd wait for the tumbling, estimate how long it would take me to get home, and predict when I would pull into the driveway. She was always correct.

The last time it happened, I called at 8:50 to say I was coming home, but the client kept me talking and I didn't actually get away until 9:10. When I arrived home I apologized for being late, and she told me she'd known in advance because Ryan didn't start tumbling until twenty minutes after I'd called!

appear for a few seconds and then disappear. Some tell us that they see the spirits of people who have passed away. Often they report feeling as if they "don't belong" or fit in with their peers, and they may also be afraid that if they confide in their parents they will be ridiculed or dismissed as "weird," as we were.

If your child came to you and said, "I see dead people," what would you do? Most parents don't know how to react to that information. They often keep quiet and hope it's just a phase the child will outgrow. We advise you to do just the opposite. Don't be afraid. Be very open to what your children are seeing or hearing, rather than dismissing it or writing it off as "just their imagination." Engage them in a dialogue, tell them that the spirit world is real, and assure them that they need not be afraid, and never, ever make them feel ashamed of sharing their unique insights with you.

Psychic children are very smart and can be extremely manipulative. What they need is structure and clear guidelines for behavior. This means combining caring with setting limits and following through with consequences if the rules are violated. Consistency is key here!

Some psychic children feel isolated because they are different from others and can't freely share their experiences. They are afraid no one will understand their unusual perceptions or feelings. As parents, therefore, it's important that you show your understanding without being too hovering and overprotective. Providing them with opportunities to express themselves creatively—such as through writing, dance, painting, acting, or music—in the company of other artistic or sensitive kids will help them develop overall confidence.

Back in the nineties, Terry had a boyfriend who was the father of two young boys, ages five and seven. We'll call them Derek and Max. Their father was very much in denial of the fact that the younger boy, Derek, had been diagnosed as autistic and that Max was very sensitive and hyperactive. It was as if acknowledging their problems would somehow reflect badly on him. Terry stepped into the role of coparent and almost immediately realized that both kids, especially Derek, were highly creative and gifted. Derek, the autistic child, would spin in circles for hours, and have screaming tantrums daily, even in school. But he loved to read comic books and draw—he made very intricate drawings. Terry encouraged him and plastered both boys' drawings all over the walls of their apartment. For the first time, these boys felt truly appreciated and started coming to life. Terry chanted with them every day (most children love chanting), and paid more attention to them than their busy working parents ever had. Derek could put his hand on Terry's forehead and read her mind. If she was visualizing a flower, he would say, "flower." He was so clairvoyant, even Terry was amazed. Month after exhausting month, she never stopped caring for and loving these two gifted children. Derek told her, "I realize you give me nothing but kindness." What planet was this psychic child from?

In time, Derek calmed down and became the smartest child in his class. By second grade, he was reading at a fifth-grade level. It was almost as though he had the mind of a savant, which fortunately Terry had recognized and nurtured. And Max also began to thrive once she was able to acknowledge and validate his emotions.

POPPY, WHY ARE YOU FLYING?

One of our clients told us this story about her intuitive twin boys:

"Poppy, why are you flying?" my three-year-old son asked my grandfather, pointing upward. His question might seem unremarkable if Poppy were a pilot, or alive. My grandfather had died the week before, and now my mother, my husband, and I stared speechless at the "empty" spot to which Geoffrey pointed. This is just one instance of many when Geoffrey and his identical twin, Connor, would point and declare, "Angel!" or "Poppy!" or "Balls of light!" On another occasion, my husband suggested taking the boys to see the manatees that flock to the warm waters surrounding a power plant. We'd never been there before, and all he said to me was, "Should we take them to see the manatees?" Connor immediately perked up and said, "Go castle!"

Because of my previous experiences with the boys' psychic awareness, I wondered whether the "castle" was a precognitive vision of the power plant. Thirty minutes later, we reached our destination, and Connor jumped from his car seat, pointed up to the plant's towering chimneys, and cried, "Castle! Go castle!"

Almost daily, we see further evidence of the boys' gifts. They seem conscious of auras, chakras, and past lives. They regularly communicate telepathically, not only with each other but also with me. They're also getting so good at reading our minds that my husband and I have trouble surprising them with birthday or Christmas presents. To me, it's all confirmation of the soul's immortality and constant expansion, and of a child's innate ability to sense it.

Indigo and Crystal Kids

James Twyman, author of *Messages from Thomas: Raising Psychic Children*, believes that we are seeing a new generation of these children among us. "For at least twenty years," he writes, "educators and scientists have realized that today's children are being born with new depths and higher perceptions.... They come into the world with the shades up and the windows polished clean.... They look at the adults in the world and say, 'Why can't you see what we see? It is so clear to us.'"

We don't know exactly why this is true, but it may simply be that their gifts are receiving more recognition than they would have a generation or two earlier. Maybe there aren't really more of them; maybe they're just emerging from the shadows and are not afraid to give voice to what they know. One consequence of this is that all highly intuitive or psychic children are now being categorized as either Indigo or Crystal, based in part on the color of their auras (the energy field that surrounds all things—we'll be talking more about auras in Chapter Five).

Part of the Indigo's purpose is to teach us how to live with more integrity. While both Crystals and Indigos are highly empathic and intuitive, Indigos tend to be more sensitive and can become depressed or upset if they are in the company of stressed or difficult people. They are "system busters" by nature—rebellious and here to change the status quo—but they are generally willing to negotiate if you offer them choices. Crystal children, on the other hand, tend to be more loving and peaceful. Their mission is to restore peace and harmony to the world. Some parents of Crystals tell us they are like baby gurus, who have wisdom beyond their years.

IS YOUR CHILD INDIGO OR CRYSTAL?

Which of the following best describes your child? (Circle all that apply.)

(a) extremely temperamental

(a) rebellious

(a) technologically oriented

(a) easily bored or irritated

(a) sometimes antisocial

(a) trailblazer

(a) verbal about expressing his needs

(b) happy and even-tempered

(b) empathic with others

(b) artistically gifted

(b) patient and loving

(b) nurturing to other children

(b) peaceful

(b) late to begin speaking

If your answers were mainly (a), you probably have an Indigo child.

If your answers were mainly (b), you probably have a Crystal child.

Both Indigo and Crystal children need to be nurtured and supported by their parents, but the way to do that may differ from one to the other.

Because Indigos are determined and strong-willed, parents need to respect them as they would adults without expecting them to take on adult responsibilities. This might mean allowing them a certain degree of autonomy and decision making, such as giving them two choices: "Do you want to wear the yellow dress or the blue dress today?" or "Would you like to go to the park or the beach this weekend?" or "Do you prefer pizza or macaroni for lunch?" This can allow them more freedom of choice and a sense that their feelings and opinions matter without burdening them with too many options at once. In addition, you must always be open and honest with them, because, like human lie detectors, they can sense when someone is not telling the truth.

Because Crystal children are so open and empathic, they may feel that it is their duty to heal other people's pain. They can easily become sad or anxious when they are in the company of sad or anxious people who, deliberately or unknowingly, use them as a dumping ground for their negative feelings. It is, therefore, extremely important that their parents help them to understand that they cannot make everything right for everyone, and that they need to protect themselves from becoming emotionally drained. (For more on psychic protection, see Chapter Five.) Try to create a safe and secure haven for them at home, a place of understanding where they can replenish themselves and regain their emotional balance.

Otherwise, for both Indigo and Crystal children, follow the advice we gave on page 23 for parenting all psychic children.

When They Reach the Teen Years

In our experience, psychic teenagers have many complex issues related to their psychic intelligence. Some teens who write to us are very depressed, because they have been too open about their gifts with the wrong people and have been judged, teased, or criticized for sharing their psychic observations. We tell teens to be cautious about sharing psychic insights, because not everyone is going to be understanding or supportive.

Also, developing teen psychics, because they don't yet understand that they are not infallible, will invariably make the mistake
of assuming that what they foresee is written in stone. Then, when
they predict something that doesn't happen, their peers can be very
critical and sometimes cruel. As a result, teen psychics can become
very self-critical, thinking, "It didn't happen as I saw it in my dream,
so I must not be a good psychic." You need to help them understand
that no psychic is perfect, and it takes many years to develop expertise. In addition, many teens are interested in ghosts and mediumship,
because they see these psychic phenomena on television shows, but
the reality can be scary for them. They may see things that are frightening, or have upsetting dreams and not know how to handle them.

Reassure your teen that having a psychic gift is normal for some
people, and not something to hide or be afraid of. Explain that different people have different talents—some may be gifted musicians or
artists, and being psychic is just another kind of gift or talent. Try to
stay open-minded and have a dialogue with your teen. Assure them
that they can always be open and honest with you, but, at the same
time, explain that their friends may not all be so open to this kind of
psychic gift and that, for their own protection, they need to be a bit
careful about how and when they share what they're experiencing.
You may want to take your teen to a psychic development class in
town, as long as the teacher is reputable. Also, this book is a good
place to start if your psychic teen is serious about developing their
abilities. The point is to be encouraging and supportive as well as
protective so that they don't shut down, as so many people do when
they reach adulthood.

What Happens When We Grow Up

Children have many natural intuitive gifts in their curiosity, openness, and sense of wonder. As adults, however, we tend to begin ques-
tioning and second-guessing ourselves. We become more self-conscious
and afraid of what others might think, and we may, therefore, lose the

courage of our convictions. We need to recapture those qualities we had as children so that we can truly open our lives to the infinite possibilities available to us. By letting go of the self-limiting beliefs that separate us from our higher dimension of self, we can recapture our power to create a better, more authentic and fulfilling life.

4

What's Getting in Your Way?

D o you envy those people who just seem to have a knack for making their lives work? They are usually the people who trust their inner knowing and have developed the intuitive sense that guides them to create better relationships and make better decisions for themselves. They are living their best, most authentic life.

We have proved over and over that we have gifts in the area of psychic abilities, but we've also spent three decades researching and developing our sixth sense. Sometimes we joke that we didn't take the road less traveled; we took the road never traveled. But with the GPS system we're going to provide, you, too, will be able to navigate through life attracting more of everything you need and want.

Let Go of Your Negativity

Those who are intuitively sensitive to other people's needs and emotions and who listen to their own inner voice often get more of what they want in life—be it more loving and fulfilling personal relationships, a more successful career, or more peace of mind—than those who rely strictly on intellect to drive their actions.

You, too, have that ability. You just need to let go of the negativity and silence the naysayer within that has been telling you to ignore your intuition. Every time you allow yourself to deny what you know, it's like clogging up a pipe with sludge. Water can't flow freely through a clogged pipe, and the negative thoughts with which you're clogging your mind are preventing your psychic intelligence from flowing as well. That negative voice is what prevents you from claiming your intuitive power. So much of the time, we get stuck in the "spin cycle," an endless tape loop of negative thoughts and feelings that paralyzes us and keeps us from moving forward. We are all like giant radio receivers fielding information on a constant basis from many different sources, and our brains are continuously filtering and interpreting what we receive. We can choose to tune in to the frequency that allows us to listen to our intuition, or we can turn the dial and pay attention to the yappy little voice that's telling us we are not psychic and the intuitive knowledge we think we have is really just a creation of our own mind.

As artists, painters, and comedians, the two of us are constantly engaged in playfully creative interactions with each other and with the people we meet every day. Sometimes we act like a couple of kids who never grew up. And, as we'll be discussing, playfulness and creativity are qualities you, too, can develop and use to shut down the negative messages you may be sending yourself, and recapture the openness to intuitive knowing that you no doubt had as a child.

Be Willing to Change

So many of us are overwhelmed in our daily lives, assaulted by so many stimuli from the external world that we shut down as a way of coping. We become emotionally numb and stubbornly resistant to change of any kind. We notice this particularly among people who grew up with an alcoholic parent or who suffered any kind of childhood trauma or abuse. Their survival mechanisms were to close themselves off emotionally. Sadly, this means that they have shut the door to their intuitive faculties as well.

There is a Buddhist expression that says, "When a person resides in hell long enough, it begins to look like a garden." We often opt for the safety of doing what's old and familiar, even if it is toxic, when doing something different would be a change for the better. Maybe that's because change always carries with it the possibility of failure, and the unknown is threatening to us. Certainly change can be risky, and sometimes scary. But if we continue to let fear of failure in the future prevent us from taking that necessary leap of faith in the here and now, we will never seize the moment we have right now to step into our greatest power. Even small, incremental changes over time can add up to a big shift. Don't expect instant results.

Twintuition Tip:
Take more risks! Learn to love living
on the edge.

Dare to Be Authentic

We spend lifetimes covering up who we really are. A friend of ours used to make big hats for theatrical costumes. He was a fiend with a hot glue gun, and if he made a mistake, he would just cover it up with a bow, a big flower, or a piece of fabric or ribbon. This approach to disguising flaws can be applied to every area of our lives. Most magazines and how-to books are focused on masking our flaws, while honing psychic intelligence is about letting go of the blocks, masks, and false beliefs we have been accumulating for years, like shedding layers of old sweaters, so that our natural abilities and deepest wisdom can emerge.

As we were writing this, we came across a magazine cover that read: LOSING IT, QUITTING IT, BEATING IT, FIGHT YOUR EATING—SHED 5 POUNDS! No wonder we're all cranky and running on empty! If you spend all your time beating, quitting, hiding, or losing something, you're constantly in a fighting frame of mind. How can that ever lead to peace of mind? Many psychic guidebooks talk about "harnessing" or "locking in" your psychic abilities as though they were rabid dogs trying to escape quarantine. We think you need to take a more relaxed approach and allow your true gifts to emerge naturally. Honing your psychic intelligence does not require a declaration of war! Be kinder and gentler with yourself, and let the process unfold.

We all carry on a constant internal dialogue based on our deepest values, beliefs, fears, and expectations. Without being aware of it, we're mentally playing a subliminal tape loop that can have a powerful influence on our self-perception and the outcomes we want to create. When you think about your desire to increase your own psychic ability, what inner dialogue is triggered by that thought? Is your immediate response, "I know I can do this. I think I could be pretty good at this!" Or is it more like, "Wow, I'd love to develop my psychic gifts, but...

- People will think I'm crazy or weird.
- People will judge me.
- People will reject me.
- I was told that it is wrong to do anything psychic.
- I won't get any psychic impressions if I try.
- I'll be disappointed in my results.
- I'll be wrong and look foolish.
- I'm not really gifted, so why try?
- I listened to my intuition once and I was wrong, so I'm probably not that good."

As you read on, we'll be giving you a variety of tactics and exercises you can use to overcome those doubts and fears and build your confidence.

START TO JOURNAL

As you begin to explore your own psyche and tap into your powers of intuition, you'll want to keep a journal where you can record your insights and keep track of your progress. Your journal doesn't have to be fancy—any kind of notebook will do—but we suggest that you find something that is aesthetically appealing to you, so that you'll be drawn to it and find pleasure in using it. And we encourage you to decorate the cover with inspiring collage images, photos, or colored markers as you would a scrapbook to make it more fun and personal.

For your first journaling exercise, write down all the negative messages you can remember having received as a child about being intuitive.

- Were you ridiculed for sharing your most cherished dreams and visions for your future with a parent or a teacher?
- Did a friend make fun of you when you shared a psychic feeling or made a prediction about something?
- Were you disrespected by a family member for having unique views or ideas that they did not agree with or understand?

Listen to your internal dialogue about those times and events. Were you made to feel embarrassed or ashamed? By whom? Did you feel sad, angry, frustrated, alienated, lonely, rejected? Like an outsider? Can you choose to react differently now? Did you create limiting beliefs based on those early experiences? Ask yourself: "Does holding on to these beliefs serve me in my daily life?"

We urge you to release anger and bitterness about past experiences that caused you to limit or judge your own intuition and sabotage the development of your gifts. Release the negative messages of parents, teachers, friends, peers, as well as those you've been sending yourself. If you're holding on to this kind of negativity, try imagining that you are holding a big colorful balloon that needs to be blown up. Take a big deep breath and blow all your negative feelings into the balloon. Now, imagine that you are tying a knot in the balloon and letting it fly away into the sky as you say to yourself, "I surrender hurt, anger, fear, and resentment."

Don't Worry So Much!

Overthinking or worrying can block psychic impressions. We get "stuck in our heads" worrying about our boss's mood, our kids' problems at school, the cute guy at the gym, what to make for dinner, or whether we remembered to lock the door when we left for work. If you find yourself in a whirlpool of negative or obsessive thoughts, say, "Stop!" out loud, and consciously dismiss the thought. Then, distract yourself. Call a friend, take a short walk, focus on a magazine article, turn on some relaxing music. One friend of ours, who happens to be a professional ballet dancer, puts on a recording of the *Alvin and the Chipmunks* theme song and dances to it! He says this works to shift his mood every time. Get out of your environment for even ten minutes and focus on your goal. Doing that will change the way you think, which will free up your energy and allow positive, optimistic thoughts to flow.

The good news is that you can change your reactions and perceptions even if you have been in a negative pattern all your life. You can make new choices about how to perceive past events and how to react in the present. Fear is a normal response to trying anything new, and one big stumbling block to expanding your psychic abilities is the tendency to minimize your talents.

> **Twintuition Tip:**
> Give yourself permission to step
> into your power.

Women especially have been taught to downplay their natural intelligence and special gifts. Our own parents were often more critical than supportive of us, and as a result, we grew up lacking confidence in ourselves even though we were brimming with passion and creativity, and it took a very long time for us to find the self-confidence we needed to become successful. We like the affirmation "I am a person of unlimited self-esteem."

We can assure you, however, that as you begin to learn and understand more about yourself and your hidden abilities, you will quiet your inner skeptic and really begin to fly.

Don't Be Afraid to Fail

Yes, as you set out on this journey of self-discovery it's important to take that leap of faith, trust yourself, trust the process, and trust the answers you receive. But you will also need to practice and sharpen your skills, just as we did. No matter how gifted you are at anything—from playing a sport or an instrument to being intuitive—you need to develop the gift you've been given. If you don't use it, you'll lose it!

Unfortunately, our schools and institutions generally reward the "right" answer, which means that we quite naturally come to believe that we need to be right all the time. And if we're not good at something right away, we tend to quit and stick to what we know we do well. As a result, the beginning intuitive will often turn early "misses" into excuses to stop trying. This is a common "rookie" mistake! Nobody ever gets better at anything without trying and missing sometimes. We urge you not to judge your first impressions as good or bad, right or wrong. Proceed gently, and keep trying. Take baby steps and know that mistakes (we prefer to call them "misinterpretations") are normal, and part of this subtle process. Let go of the compulsive need to be perfect or "spot on" with every psychic impression or prediction. Give yourself permission to be "wrong," to misinterpret signs. "Dare to be lousy!" as one of our painting teachers used to say. Part of the process is learning to embrace your humanness and releasing the perfectionist within you that has to be "right" or measure up to some impossible standard. Think of this as a fun journey or exploration into the esoteric and transcendent regions of your psyche.

JOGGIN' YOUR NOGGIN:
A BRAINSTORMING EXERCISE TO HELP INCREASE YOUR INTUITION

Try this with a group of friends or by yourself to see how "brainstorming" can increase your intuitive creativity.

Begin with a problem or question to which you would like to find an answer and just let your creativity run wild. There are just three rules for brainstorming to find the answer to any question or problem:

1. There is to be no criticism or judgment of any ideas presented.
2. Quantity is desirable; the more ideas the better.
3. No idea is too bizarre, too wild, or too irrelevant. The purpose is not to be correct but to fuel the process of generating imaginative alternatives.

If you are alone, you'll have to act as leader, note-taker, and group. Since the act of writing can interfere with the flow of ideas, however, you might want to use a tape recorder. At the end of the session see how many creative new solutions you've come up with. We think you'll be surprised.

Trust in Yourself

We were very hard on ourselves in the first years of our psychic work, putting way too much pressure on ourselves to be like human computers and "know everything"—as if such a thing were even possible! Looking back, we realize that, because we had no training and no available role models, we had ridiculously unrealistic expectations of what it meant to be psychic. (It didn't help that we were extreme perfectionists!) In some ways, however, that was actually a good thing because we didn't limit ourselves to what anyone else said we

could or couldn't do or how we should do it; to us, anything was possible. We were—and still are—able to ignore anyone who told us we
couldn't do something just because it had never been done before. We
were "spirit taught," which means we relied solely on the guidance of
our spirit teachers in other dimensions. (We'll be talking more about
those in Chapter Eleven.)

Once, when someone asked us, "What makes you think you can
predict the future?" we responded, "Why can't we? We never put
limits on what we can do." As Capricorns, we are true mountain goats
who love scaling the steepest cliffs—in fact, we thrive on challenge!
We realize that what we are doing has never been done before in quite
the way we are doing it, and in that sense, we are pioneers. We believe
in the old Chinese proverb: "He who believes a thing cannot be done
should get out of the way of the person who is doing it." Even more
important: Get out of your *own* way!

We know what you're thinking—that's easy to say but maybe
not so easy to do. But it's really easier than you think, and in the next
chapter we'll be giving you all kinds of exercises, tips, and strategies
you can use to help you get out of your own way.

Learn to Tap into Your Power

To enhance your psychic intelligence, you need to take care of yourself in body, mind, and spirit. If you neglect any one aspect of your life, the others will also suffer.

To take better care of your mind and spirit, we recommend doing more things that you really enjoy and fewer things you think you "should" do. Engage in more creative activities like writing, dancing, singing, or painting. Engage in positive self-talk to affirm your psychic abilities (see discussion of affirmations on pages 47–48). Get more in touch with your emotions, open your heart, and stop judging yourself and others. Even baby steps can make a big difference. Make a conscious effort to be more loving and patient.

To nurture your body, try to slow down. Don't overcommit. If you are shuttling your kids to fifteen sports activities, cut them down to seven. Your kids will thank you and so will your body! During the day, check in with yourself and your body. Are you holding tension in your neck? Do you have a feeling of dread or sadness in your stomach? Learn to set healthy boundaries without feeling guilty. Get plenty of sleep and nourish yourself with healthy foods.

This chapter will talk about how to implement these healthy changes and more.

What Kind of Energy Do You Give Out?

The energies of our bodies and our world are constantly fluctuating. Each of us is surrounded by an electromagnetic field, also known as an "aura," that contains the information and vibrational energy we are sending out to the world on a continuous basis. Our aura colors reflect our thoughts and emotions and are strong indicators of our physical and spiritual health. Therefore, knowing the color of your aura can help you to determine what kinds of vibrations you're sending. Changing your thoughts and feelings—about yourself and the world—as well as your physical health, will create a corresponding change in your aura.

While there are many shades of color and, therefore, shades of meaning in people's auras, these are the ten basic colors and what they have to say:

> *RED:* The color of blood, red indicates strength, physical and sexual energy, a vital life force and strong will, as well as passion and courage.
>
> *ORANGE:* The color of opportunity, orange also shows creativity, organization, adaptability, and a feeling for the needs of others.
>
> *YELLOW:* The color of the sun, yellow indicates energy, vitality, intellect, prosperity, playfulness, optimism, and the ability to communicate.
>
> *GREEN:* The color of nature and ecology, green indicates growth, change, and healing, as well as prosperity, fertility, and new beginnings.
>
> *BLUE:* Indicates peace, tranquility, healing, caring for others, compassion, and verbal communication.
>
> *PURPLE:* The color of passion and magic, purple or violet is also symbolic of spirituality, psychic power, and clairvoyance.
>
> *WHITE:* The color of protection and spirituality, innocence and purity.

BROWN: The color of the soil, brown indicates stability, grounding, practicality, and an emphasis on the physical, perhaps at
the expense of the spiritual.

SILVER: Indicates clarity of purpose.

GOLD: The color of spiritual energy and inspiration.

What Color Is Your Aura?

There is a process known as "Kirlian photography" (named for its
inventor, Semyon Kirlian) that involves photographing subjects in
the presence of a high-frequency energy field to obtain an image that
shows multicolored auric emanations. In addition, some people just
have a natural gift for seeing their own and other people's auras. But

PRACTICE SEEING OTHER PEOPLE'S AURAS

We sometimes capture the color of a subject's aura in our automatic
writing, and people who are spiritual artists paint aura colors they see
in their mind's eye. Here's an exercise that will help you learn to see
other people's auras.

Ask the person whose aura you are reading to stand against a blank
white wall. Make sure there is plenty of light and that there are no shadows being cast on the wall. Squint and try to observe a color or energy
around the person. You may see several different colors. Share these
colors with your partner, along with any feelings or observations you
may have picked up while you were looking at him or her. Then discuss
the meaning of what you've observed. If you're successful on your first
attempt, it's probably a sign that clairvoyance is your strongest Clair (for
more on clairvoyance, see Chapter Seven). If you observed no colors at
all, don't be upset. The more you do this, the more you'll be able to see.
Keep practicing. Over time you'll find that you are able to make connections between a person's feelings or personality and his or her aura
colors.

you can also practice seeing the color of your aura. All you need to do is stand in front of a mirror and focus on the outline of your body for three to four minutes a day. At first you may see nothing, but in time you'll see colors or shimmering energy emerging. Record any colors or perceptions in your journal. Continue to do this as you practice tuning in to your psychic intelligence, and note any changes that occur. You'll begin to see how the changing colors correspond to the changes in your feelings and thoughts.

Examine Your Fears

We've talked about the fact that, as you begin your journey of self-discovery, you'll have to overcome your fear and take a leap of faith. But in addition to fear of the unknown, you may have other fears and emotional baggage that are preventing you from tuning in to your inner voice and receiving higher guidance. Some fears are totally rational and serve to protect us from harm. The problem is that many of us never examine our fears to determine whether they are actually serving us in any way. When we begin to do that, we may notice a pattern of self-sabotage or limiting beliefs we weren't even aware of that could be blocking access to our psychic intelligence.

JOURNALING EXERCISE: WHAT ARE YOU AFRAID OF?

Take some time to think about what your fears might be. Then get out your journal and write them down. Here are a few examples:

I am afraid that I won't be able to support my family.
I am afraid of trusting my decisions.
I am afraid that I will be alone as I get older.
I am afraid that something bad will happen to my children.
I am afraid of being judged.

Now it's your turn:

I am afraid _____.
I am afraid _____.
I am afraid _____.

Take as much time and as much room as you need. Now write an affirmation that refutes each of these fears. For example:

I easily support my family.
I trust my decisions. I make good decisions.
I will always be surrounded by good and loving friends. I will never
    be alone.
I know that my children are safe.
There will always be critics. I live my life freely, independent of the
    opinions of others.

The more you affirm the opposite of whatever you fear, the more easily you'll be able to refute and let go of your fears.

View the World from a New Perspective

Many of us have a tendency to use fear and self-doubt as an excuse to play it safe and avoid taking risks.

The two of us had to overcome extreme shyness and stage fright when we first started performing. Terry in particular had trouble remembering parts of our comedy act, and Linda would jump in to rescue her. But we continued challenging these fears and phobias until we conquered them. The anxiety didn't completely go away, but it doesn't control us anymore. You, too, can determine to challenge the negative inner voice that says you have no options, no possibilities.

A friend of ours once told us that self-doubt and fear had undermined her desire to be truly psychic for most of her life. As a result, she became too dependent on everyone's opinion but her own. We all have doubts when we begin this work of self-discovery, but we can choose to commit to being greater than our fears and to viewing the world from a new perspective.

In this cynical culture it is difficult to allow ourselves to feel vulnerable and expose a softer side of our personalities. Cynicism is an easy way to cover up fear. It may be cool, funny, and hip to dismiss or debunk what we can't or don't want to understand, but what we need to do is face down our fears rather than deny them. As one of our favorite writers, Florence Scovel Shinn, wrote in *The Game of Life and How to Play It*, "Nothing stands between man and his highest ideals and every desire of his heart but doubt and fear. When man can 'wish without worrying,' every desire will be instantly fulfilled." We couldn't agree more!

Letting go of fear does not mean that you are always going to feel confident. It means that you are choosing to trust in yourself and have faith in a power greater than yourself. The brilliant actor Christopher Walken once said on television, "I think that if someone is confident all the time, there is something wrong with him." While this is funny, it is also true that most of us think we should feel confident all the time (or at least *act* like we do). Yet, as humans, this is putting way too much pressure on ourselves.

When you're afraid, you may be disconnected from the inner wisdom or source energy that could help you solve the problem. You don't know what to do, and you panic. When you feel yourself beginning to panic, we urge you to focus on your breath and repeat to yourself, "I am safe. I trust that the solution will come. It's on its way." Often the answer or solution will come in a very simple way. You may hear, feel, or know what to do. The more you trust your psychic intelligence to provide you with the best decision, the less fear you will feel and the more centered you will be when a crisis arises. Ask your inner guide for the wisest course of action and trust your psychic intelligence to provide you with the best decision in that moment.

THREE STRATEGIES FOR RELEASING YOUR FEAR

1. Think of someone whose confidence you admire and imagine what choice he or she would make in your situation. Try to act as if you were that same confident person.
2. Instead of worrying about what other people think of your choices, take a deep breath, focus your thoughts, and repeat to yourself that the choices you are making have the power to create positive transformation. Once you adopt that perspective, you will no longer have to fear the disbelief or disapproval of others.
3. Ask yourself: "How do I want to *feel* right now?" Get out your journal and begin to write words that inspire, soothe, or comfort you. Do you want to feel enthusiastic? Grateful? Humble? Free? Empowered? Accomplished? Inspired? Connected? Exhilarated? Important? Joyful? Intuitive? Wise? Dynamic? Let your mind run free and don't censor your thoughts or feelings.

Eat, Pray, Duck! Avoiding the Karmic Boomerang

When we are holding on to the past, we are staying attached to negative energy that keeps us from moving forward. Every one of us can bring more of what we want into our life, but to do that we need to embrace the idea of change.

The two of us practice chanting as a way to release unhealthy bonds to past feelings and experiences of which we may be totally unaware. For more than twenty-five years we have embraced a form of Japanese Buddhism called Nichiren Daishonin Buddhism, which is based on the belief that we all can attain what is called a state of enlightenment through "karmic expiation" in our present lifetime. What this means is that we can make new choices that will, in effect, right the wrongs we may have created in the past and, in so doing, change our destiny. Once we have wiped the karmic slate clean, we can create our lives from the perspective of a new intention, not from the past or someone else's agenda.

The primary practice of this form of Buddhism is to chant the words *"nam myoho renge kyo,"* as we do every morning and every evening. This mantra is Shakyamuni Buddha's highest teaching and the title of the Lotus Sutra. It translates as, "I devote my life to the Mystic Law of Cause and Effect through the sutra, or teaching, of the Buddha." The Mystic Law is the fundamental principle of the Universe. *Renge* (pronounced ren-gay) symbolizes the lotus flower, which blossoms and seeds at the same time, representing the simultaneity of cause and effect. In Buddhism, as well as Hinduism, every action has consequences—an equal reaction—some immediate and some delayed. Lessons not learned in our present life must be learned in the next one. By the same token, the good actions we take in the present will impact our future incarnations.

Western scholars have mistakenly confused "karma" with "fate." Fate is actually the belief that one's life path is created by agencies outside oneself. Karma (which literally means "action") is a law of compensation. It means that what you sow you will reap. We have control of what we sow and, therefore, by changing our actions and our reactions (which generally means also changing our thoughts), we are able to change our destiny. In Buddhism, this is often referred to as "getting off the wheel of karma," because, instead of going around and around in the same circle, we can choose to move in a different direction. If we don't change (or move out of the way), we risk getting hit in the head with the karmic boomerang.

Minute by minute, we are each choosing either to open up and receive good experiences or to stay closed off and stuck in anger, frustration, or fear. As we've already discussed, we always have a choice. The future is fluid. We all have free will and we can change our own destiny. But to do that we must embrace change. That's what developing our intuition is all about. It is about perceiving a different— and more effective—solution to a problem.

Use Obstacles to Create Opportunity

Since obstacles are inevitably a part of life, we might as well use them as fuel for our enlightenment. There's an old Chinese proverb that says, "Crisis is opportunity." The problem, however, is that most of us tend to see the crisis but not the opportunity. If you can think of your life as an adventure in spiritual development, your problems will become interesting opportunities to change your karma by acting (or thinking) differently.

The True Buddha Nichiren Daishonin told a story called "The Dragon Gate" in which a school of carp is swimming upstream against the current. They make it partway, but most of the carp eventually give up and swim back. Those that keep trying, however, become dragons. Applying this lesson to overcoming your fears in order to develop your psychic intelligence, it means that, in the end, the benefits you receive will be even more valuable than what you could have imagined.

Use Affirmations to Cement the Power of Your Intention

Using affirmations is an extremely powerful way to release your fears and harness the power of your intention to pull into your life more of what is positive. The word "affirmation" means "the assertion of the truth or existence of something." Affirmations are strong, declarative statements (also called "self-talk") that assert a new belief or thought about yourself that will translate into a new way of being.

Whether you use the ones listed below or make up your own, your statements must be in the present tense—as if they were true right now—and you must focus the power of your mind on experiencing them as true. If you say one thing while thinking another, your thoughts will overpower your words because it is your thoughts that create your reality. Also, they must be worded in the positive, which means avoiding negative words like "not." The reason for this is that your subconscious does not register negatives, so if, for example, you state, "I will not be afraid," what your subconscious hears is "I will be afraid." Not exactly what you were hoping to affirm!

As you say the words, picture yourself as a superhero like Iron Man or Wonder Woman taking charge and moving forward confidently. Hold on to the feelings that this picture brings up for you as you repeat your affirmation. Over the years, we've found affirmations extremely helpful for changing negative beliefs to positive beliefs. But they will only work if you put the power of intention into your words and repeat them consistently so that they are internalized.

One affirmation we particularly like is: "I am the creator of my experiences. I am creating a life full of joy, creativity, purpose, and aliveness." Remember, you are the designer and architect of your future.

Here are a few more affirmations you might use to help you let go of your fears:

- I am bigger than my fears.
- I release fear and negativity.
- I am safe and protected.
- It is safe for me to open myself to spiritual guidance.
- I am willing to risk opening myself to my true potential.
- As I identify my fears, I replace them with new intentions.
- I trust my inner guidance system to assist me.
- The Universe supports me.
- I trust that the best options and solutions will be presented.
- I am safe.

Nurture Your Body to Enhance Your Intuition

Remember that your mind, body, and spirit are all related, so what's healthy for one of these three aspects of your being will enhance the health of the other two as well.

Our body is the instrument we use for channeling energies, so we really need to keep it as pure a vessel as possible. Some psychics are vegetarians, but that may not work for you, and we don't feel it's necessary for everyone. However, a toxic diet can clog the "filter" that allows you to discern fine shades of meaning as you interpret psychic messages, and, therefore, negatively impact your psychic work. If you are toxic, your channel or "conduit" will simply not be clear. We'll have an occasional martini or a beer now and then, but we know that drinking a lot of alcohol or using drugs will block our intuition, as will eating junk food. You want to maintain a clear vibration.

To purify your body and clear the way for receiving psychic messages, we suggest that you:

- Eat lots of fresh organic fruits and vegetables.
- Avoid pesticides.
- Limit alcohol intake.
- Exercise and lift weights thirty minutes per day.
- Eat a high fiber diet.
- Decrease your intake of beef and pork.
- Do not smoke.
- Cut back on processed foods and "junk" foods.
- Always avoid trans-fatty acids.
- Take vitamin supplements with folic acid and selenium.
- Decrease your intake of fatty foods.
- Avoid overuse of antibiotics.
- Replace all cooking oils with olive oil or canola oil.
- Watch your weight.
- Drink at least six glasses of water a day.
- Eat foods rich in antioxidants.
- Cut back on sugars and soft drinks.

Junk Takes Up Room in Your Head and Your Heart

Over the years, we've learned to let go of all kinds of things and behaviors, thoughts and beliefs that no longer work for us.

To do your own "interior redecorating," you need to rearrange your mental furniture. Put a coat of fresh paint on the walls of your mind. Go through the closets and drawers and mentally toss out old ideas and painful memories. Doing what we call a mental makeover will bring you more peace of mind and a new outlook on life.

As you begin to open your mind and listen to your psychic voice, you need to ask yourself not only, "What am I willing to let go of?" but also "*Who* am I willing to let go of?" Is your boyfriend a no-good slob who mooches off you and spends all your money on hot wings and beer? Is your boss a raving menopausal lunatic who downloads her rage on you?

Sometimes we cling to old, outworn, ill-fitting relationships the same way we hold on to our old clothes. But there's a significant

JOURNALING EXERCISE: DUMP YOUR EMOTIONAL BAGGAGE

Some of us get so used to carrying the weight of the world on our shoulders that we don't even stop to question the burdens we carry. Airlines are charging for every bag you check or carry on. Can you imagine if airlines started charging fees for emotional baggage? The planes would never get off the ground!

If you're feeling weighed down mentally and emotionally, get out your journal and ask yourself the following questions:

- Is there someone I need to forgive? Why?
- Am I beating myself up for missing an opportunity? What is the payoff?

- Do I need to forgive myself for something?
- In what way is this belief, habit, or obsession holding me back?
- What do I think I could accomplish if I released it?
- Am I angry with someone? Who?
- How would I feel if I could let go of that anger?
- Is there an experience in my life I wish I could forget? What?
- Am I being true to myself?
- Am I holding on to a secret?
- Am I willing to continue living with my secrets?

If you find that you're holding on to emotional baggage from the past, it's time to forgive and move on. Remember the law of karma: You can always *choose* to change the way you act and/or react, and by doing that you are choosing to change your future. Holding on to a grudge is like taking poison and then waiting for someone else to die. You are the one who suffers! It is time to let go and free yourself. Forgiveness does not mean that the other person is without fault, or that you condone his or her behavior; you forgive so you can move on unencumbered. Depending on the situation, you may want to talk to a counselor about your past traumas. When you are ready, say a prayer of thanks for the experience. You are learning tolerance, appreciation, and acceptance.

difference. Unlike people, our old clothes aren't making any demands on us. They're not hanging there in the closet screaming, "Wear me! Pay attention to me!" They're not taking an emotional toll. If you're allowing yourself to become a punching bag for someone else's anger or trying to solve everyone's problems but your own, it's time to set some boundaries and separate yourself from their negativity.

Jettison Your Physical Junk

Okay, so you've determined to let go of all the negative thoughts and emotions that may be weighing you down and preventing you from moving forward with your life. Now you also need to get rid of all the physical stuff you don't need that's taking up room in your life.

Junk comes in many forms, but basically it's stuff you're hanging on to that you don't need and that is probably weighing you down. Truthfully, we come from a family of collectors (some would say "hoarders"). Our mother held on to decades-old clothes including Bermuda shorts and circle skirts. She saved our old dolls and stuffed animals as well as her outdated lipsticks and Christmas cards from people who had died years ago. She had lists and lists of things to do that never got done, and, interestingly, one of her main complaints was that she felt bored, trapped, and stuck.

Our dad admits that he has to hold on to everything he ever acquired. He still has the fake trout mounted on a plaque that sings "Don't Worry, Be Happy," which we gave him about twenty years ago and has had no effect whatsoever on his tendency to worry.

Our brother, Flip, who rebuilds musical instruments, has two houses filled with vintage pianos, nickelodeons, pipe organs, and obscure instruments of every kind. And now that he's started collecting and restoring vintage French sports cars, he's borrowing more space from his friends to store his cars!

> That's all you need in life, a little place for your stuff.
> That's all your house is: a place to keep your stuff. If you
> didn't have so much stuff, you wouldn't need a house.
> You could just walk around all the time. A house is just
> a pile of stuff with a cover on it.
> —George Carlin

We, too, have the collecting habit, but since we share a modest two-bedroom apartment, we've been forced to control our tendency to hoard. Not so long ago, it had gotten to the point where our closets were overflowing, and the boxes of notes, books, scraps of paper with half-formed ideas, and old VHS tapes were getting out of hand. So we bit the bullet, hired an assistant, and got it all organized. As soon as the space was cleared, we began to receive requests for television appearances and print interviews, and we attacked our writing with renewed vigor. Suddenly, our creativity was on fire!

Hold Your Own Clearance Sale

We suggest that you try it; you'll be amazed by how liberating the experience can be. If for some reason you're afraid to let go, ask yourself the following questions:

- What do I hope to change or accomplish by jettisoning my junk?
- What will be the mental payoff?
- What will be the emotional payoff?
- What has been the emotional toll of holding on to all this stuff?
- How do I want to feel: free, light, open, powerful, flexible, spacious, creative, inspired?
- How do I want my home to look?
- What is the first closet or drawer I want to tackle?
- What stuff do I most need to unload?

After you have gone through the first closet, pick another. Or clean out a drawer—any drawer. Notice how it gets easier as you go along. Do you really need a hundred pairs of mismatched socks? Or five red leather wallets your mother gave you that you couldn't bring yourself to part with? Or the Martian brain disintegrator from little Joey's sixth birthday? Joey is thirty-eight now....

What are your fears? Stresses? Excuses? What do you think will happen if you let go of the baggage that's weighing you down and allow your psychic self to soar? Will you be judged, ridiculed, or rejected by your family or friends? Will you be opening yourself up to negative energies or even frightening experiences?

JOURNALING EXERCISE: WHAT AM I WILLING TO LET GO?

Get out your journal and at the top of a clean page make five columns labeled:

Work   Relationships   Beliefs   Family   Diet

List what you need to let go of in each category. An example might be: "I need to let go of being all things to all people on the job," or "I need to stop drinking those deluxe double-caramel mochaccinos with extra whipped cream."

Check your list regularly to monitor your progress. Realize that sometimes you may backslide, and that's okay. Don't expect overnight success—please be patient with yourself. (In fact, if what you expect of yourself is perfection, you might want to add letting go of the need to be perfect to your list.)

Psychic Self-Defense: Protect Yourself from Negativity

It's not always possible to separate yourself entirely from every negative person in your life, but you can protect yourself from absorbing and being affected by the negativity of others. This is known as "psychic protection."

Have you ever dated someone and wondered why you felt totally depressed after the date? Do you notice that you are extremely tired when you are in the company of a particular family member, friend, or coworker?

People who, intentionally or unintentionally, steal or "suck" the energy from positive people are generally known as "psychic vampires." Other terms for this type of person include "energy vampire," "energy predator," and "energy parasite" because they leave you feeling exhausted, depressed, or just plain weird. (By the same token, of course, you can feel uplifted or energized by being in the vibration of a child or a happy person.)

> **Twintuition Tip:**
> Don't be a psychic vacuum for other people's negativity.

Sensitive people subconsciously want to transmute or heal the negativity of others who are in pain or who are suffering emotionally. This is certainly an empathic impulse, but it can lead to unhealthy co-dependencies, and it's almost always the one who is taking on the pain of the other who ultimately pays the price. So tune in to how you feel when you spend time with the various people in your life, and how you feel afterward. Take your emotional temperature. Do you feel tense, anxious, drained, or dispirited? Do you have a friend who calls only to download her problems on you? Some people are addicted to complaining and never take your advice anyway. Is your significant other passive-aggressive or covertly hostile? A covertly hostile person is called a "suppressive." You may find that you feel very tired or become more accident-prone when you're around the energy of a suppressive person. These people are often unaware of the negative effects they have on others. It may help to have an honest conversation with the negative person about how his or her behavior makes you feel. Own your feelings so that you are not blaming, just sharing. For example, instead of "You're always criticizing me," say: "When you are critical of me, it makes me feel that you don't respect me." Then ask the person for what you need from him or her. Say: "What I would like from you is to have your support in my new [project, relationship, path of study, etc.]." Enroll this person in supporting you by being honest about what you need. Not only will you feel dramatically better, but you'll notice that your intuition will start to kick into high gear!

Sometimes, however, there will be a toxic or negative person in your life who is unwilling or unable to change. What you need to do then is disconnect from that person, or—if that isn't possible (because he or she is a close relative, a boss, or a coworker)—at least try to limit your exposure to his or her negative energy. Our friend Larry wears a T-shirt that says sarcastically, "Let me just drop everything and focus on *your* problem." There are plenty of people out there who think we should do just that. They can be very demanding, and we need to set boundaries with everyone in our life and be very clear about what we are willing to do, how much time and energy we give to each person. Firmly state, "I can't do that," or "I just have too much on my plate, I'm sorry." It may take some practice, but we need to remain centered and focused so that we don't absorb or pick up on other people's neediness and negativity. Too many of us don't know who we really are, and in our quest for approval we are easily swayed by the demands and expectations of others.

Try to keep your thoughts positive and peaceful when you are around toxic people. Don't let another person make you feel bad. If you are empathic, you may be a virtual sponge, absorbing the feelings, worry, and anger of other people. Remember, you are the only one in control of your emotions because you are the only one who can decide to react or not to react. Take a moment to step back and look at things from another perspective. Try your best to understand where the negative person is coming from. Most often it is a place of hurt and anger that probably has absolutely nothing to do with you.

Not so long ago, Linda received an e-mail from an acquaintance named Elissa whom she'd run into at the home of a mutual friend. Here's what she wrote:

> When we were talking the other day and, in the middle of the conversation, you told me that I am an empath, it really caught me by surprise. Suddenly everything made a lot of sense. In that very moment, you clarified to me what had left me dumbfounded for years. I had always been told by friends and family that I was "too emotional" and that I needed to "get a grip." Sometimes I would have a wave of sadness wash

over me and not have the slightest clue as to why. When you uttered those words to me, a huge relief came over me and I knew to my core that you were one hundred percent correct. All of those years wondering why I would suddenly become sad or distraught made perfect sense: I was picking up on the emotions of other people around me. You gave me a great gift that afternoon: clarity. I am forever thankful!

Go within and tune in to your feelings and higher voice. Our intuition speaks to us through insights, impressions, symbols, or divine whispers. Sometimes you need to hear the message several times before you take the hint. "The gods tend to whisper before they scream," a wise man once said. The more you become attuned to those whisperings, the better able you'll be to protect yourself before someone else's negativity can cause you serious psychic harm. Once you learn new ways to maintain your own safe space, you will feel empowered and your intuitive energy will easily start to flow! As you raise your vibration and become more spiritual, you will notice that negative people start to fall away naturally and look for a more willing victim to feed on.

Use Psychic Protection Tools

If you find that a psychic vampire is sapping your positive energy, there are steps you can take to clear your aura and get your energy flowing again. Here are a few methods we've found to be the most effective psychic protection techniques:

- Imagine yourself surrounded by mirrors that reflect the negativity of others back at them.
- Imagine yourself surrounded by a shield of gold (for spiritual energy and inspiration), white (the color of protection), or silver (for clarity of purpose) light. Repeat to yourself, "I am safe and protected from any negative person, energy, or experience." Or, "I attract only positive experiences and people."

- Call upon Archangel Michael (considered the commander-in-chief of God's army), or the archangel with whom you feel most connected, and ask him to protect you from the negative energy of the people with whom you interacted that particular day.
- Exercise to get your psychic energy flowing!
- Spend time in nature, especially in the sun, to keep yourself focused and grounded.
- Essential oils such as jasmine and rose oil, frankincense, lavender, eucalyptus, honeysuckle, and sage can help clear your aura and your mind. Put no more than a drop or two in a lotion or bath, because their energies can be strong. This can activate the chakras or energy centers. (For more on chakras, see pages 71–73.) Many healers use these oils.
- Add two to three tablespoons of Epsom salts, Dead Sea salts, or sea salt to your bathwater for healing and cleansing.
- Imagine that you are standing under a waterfall of pink rose quartz light that flows through, down, and around you. Pink rose quartz crystal is generally believed to have a soothing and healing energy.
- Imagine that you are going through a car wash; then zip yourself into a cocoon of white (protective) light.
- Maintain a positive attitude and focus on happy feelings. Remember that what you focus on will expand!
- Quickly sweep your hands from the crown of your head down the front of your body. Then sweep the palms of your hands down each arm, as if brushing off your sleeves, from your shoulders down past your fingertips. This will clear your chakras or energy centers. Try putting your feet in a pan filled with a half-inch layer of salt to draw the negative or blocked energies out of your body. If you have a garden you can also put your bare feet in soil to help reground yourself, or soak them in warm water with a few drops of lavender or another essential oil. Relax and close your eyes for five or ten minutes.

USE SMUDGING TO CLEAR NEGATIVE ENERGY

Negative people leave a dark cloud of toxic energy in their wake. Smudging is a traditional way to clear out that residual energy. Although it has been practiced all over the world, smudging is most closely associated with Native American rituals used to drive away negative energy.

You will need a bundle of herbs (usually dried sage leaves, but frankincense, sandalwood, or myrrh are also effective) known as a "smudge stick," and a small bowl. Smudge sticks are easy to make and you can find instructions at various websites. Light the tip of the herb bundle until it starts to smoke. Then walk around your home, or the entire area you want to clear, using your hand to waft the smoke in all directions while you ask the spirit world to restore peace and balance to the space. When you are done, thank your spirit guides for watching over you and take a moment to notice how different and how much "lighter" the energy of your environment now feels. And it smells wonderful, too!

Twintuition Tip:
Imagine that you're wearing a kind of body glove that deflects negative or toxic energy so that you don't absorb it.

Find Your Passion and Be Willing to Dream

Back in the eighties we took a self-improvement seminar called The Forum during which participants were asked to state what about themselves they were trying to change. When Terry stood up and stated that she was trying to "understand joy," the entire roomful of two hundred people cracked up! Joy is a feeling we had little concept of at that time. And the reason everyone was laughing was that they could relate to Terry's dilemma. It almost seems too simple: doing things you love equals the feeling of joy. Yet that is truly the recipe for joy, and it can also lead to a heightened sense of awareness, the key to intuition.

Few people these days make time for fun, hobbies, or artistic activities. When we first attempted to do things "just to feel good," we actually felt guilty about taking the time away from work. Many people feel this way and you may, too. Feeling good? What a foreign concept! But it wasn't until we made a regular habit of doing things we loved, even if we earned no money doing them, that the answers to all our hopes and dreams started coming our way—as they continue to do to this day. The problem is, most of us don't know what our passions are, and we have even less of an idea of what things make us happy or feel good.

In his book *Wherever You Go, There You Are: Mindfulness Meditation in Everyday Life*, Jon Kabat-Zinn writes that the one question we should be asking ourselves over and over is "What is my job on the planet?" Once we find the answer to that question, we will know what brings us true joy. Many of us think of our job as something we *have* to do in order to be able to do the things we really *want* to do. But if we're living authentically and doing the job we were meant to do, our job and our joy will be synonymous.

JOURNALING EXERCISE: WHAT'S IMPORTANT TO YOU?

Get out your journal and ask yourself: "What is really important to me?" Make a list of all the things you've wanted to do but haven't yet tried— because you were afraid, because you didn't think you had the time, because you thought you couldn't, or maybe because you just didn't think you were worth it. We can all come up with a million reasons for *not* doing something—especially if we think it's something impractical.

Too often, when we ask people to name something they've always wanted to do or try, they can't come up with one single thing. You'd think that meant they've done everything they've ever wanted to do—that they're completely fulfilled. And for a very few, that could be true. But most often it really means that they can't think of anything they feel passionate about, and we think that's sad. We want you to find your passion, have more fun, become more imaginative and creative—more alive. Once you start doing new things, you'll be opening up your mind to new beliefs and abilities you never knew you had. You'll be getting back to that childlike place where you believed you had the power to make anything happen.

Start right now by making a list of five things you have always wanted to do.

I want to:

1. _____.
2. _____.
3. _____.
4. _____.
5. _____.

If you can't think of anything, ask yourself this question: "How do I want to feel?" Now imagine yourself engaged in various activities and see which one makes you feel the way you want to. Let your mind run free and don't censor your wish list. After all, if you're dreaming, you might as well dream big!

Start Getting Creative

As you begin to visualize a new way of being, a new identity that is different from your old one, give yourself permission to explore creative channels you may have been too shy, too embarrassed, or too scared to try. Studies have shown that the brain feeds on novelty. If you are too mired in routine, you may be shutting off the intuitive areas of your brain. Doing something new stimulates different parts of the brain and enhances learning and memory skills. If you work with numbers or computers all day, try juggling or abstract painting. If you are a writer, try playing number games that challenge you to make new cognitive connections. If you do crossword puzzles, try sudoku. Changing up your activities can develop and strengthen the psychic regions of your brain. Start a short story about your children. Plant a pot of cheerful red geraniums or a container garden with herbs. Try a new casserole recipe, using ingredients that you don't normally use.

Would you like to learn to tango or tap dance? Play flamenco guitar? Enroll in an art class or singing class? Join an improv comedy group? Take up the didgeridoo? Whatever it is, give yourself permission to try it, and then make it happen. No one is asking you to become a master painter or a great dramatic actor—in fact, no one even has to know. Engaging in a creative or artistic activity is a great way to let go of your rational left brain, expand your intuitive right brain, and increase the scope of your psychic intelligence.

WHAT YOUR RIGHT BRAIN KNOWS THAT YOUR LEFT BRAIN DOESN'T

It was neurobiologist Roger Sperry who first determined that the left and right hemispheres of the brain have distinct functions and are responsible for two different ways of thinking. We need both in our lives, but too many of us have become so left-brain oriented that we ignore or shut down our right brain completely. To access our intuition, we need to reopen that channel and allow the information to flow freely.

The Left Brain Is	The Right Brain Is
Logical	Random
Sequential	Intuitive
Rational	Holistic
Analytical	Synthesizing
Objective	Subjective

Very often when we suggest that a client "go paint something," his or her immediate response is to protest, "Oh, no, I can't draw!" But that's not the point. What we want you to do is give yourself permission to let go of your inhibitions and make a big colorful mess! Line your kitchen table with newspaper if you have to and paint away—the way you did when you were little. Children don't care if they stay within the lines. They make trees purple and the sky pink if they want to. And that's the kind of creative freedom we're asking you to embrace. Allow yourself to feel free and have fun with bright colors. Do you always dress in beige, gray, or neutrals? Boring! Add some pizzazz to your wardrobe with a bright turquoise blouse or a lemon-yellow scarf. A bold pop of color can really pick up your mood, make you feel more powerful, and affect how others respond to you. There is so much healing power in color.

> Every child is an artist. The problem is how to
> remain an artist once we grow up.
> —Pablo Picasso

Drawing is a skill that requires us to integrate several modes of perception—seeing edges, spaces, relationships—into an integrated whole. Betty Edwards, author of *Drawing on the Right Side of the Brain,* talks about the fact that being able to draw requires our being able to "see" objects differently from the way we generally perceive them. And that, in turn, means being able to disorient our analytical, left-brain mode of perception so that we are more or less forced to use our more creative and intuitive right-brain way of seeing. To help her students do this, she devised an exercise that required them to look at a familiar image upside-down and copy it. By doing that, they were forced to see the familiar in an entirely new way—which is exactly how we're asking you to look at your life, your desires, your passions, and your intuitive abilities.

Or maybe music is your thing. While it would be great if you could play an instrument (even badly), just listening to music is also a way to expand your intuition. Listening to music is an all-encompassing experience in which the sound envelops and surrounds us. We don't concentrate on analyzing one instrument or another; we allow all the parts to synthesize into a transcendent whole. Einstein once said when speaking about how he came to arrive at his theory of relativity, "It occurred to me by intuition, and music was the driving force behind that intuition. My discovery was the result of musical perception."

For most of our lives we are taught to come up with the "right" answer and to dismiss all other possible answers as "wrong." But life isn't a multiple-choice exam, and allowing your intuitive right brain the freedom to experiment is one of the best ways there is to open yourself up to new possibilities and deeper truths about yourself.

Psychic Dos and Don'ts

As you move ahead developing your psychic intelligence, here are a few tips to keep in mind:

DO
- Put yourself at the top of your to-do list.
- Try new things! Shake up your routine.
- Carve out time for your hobby or passion every day.
- Pay attention to your feelings.
- Set boundaries with family and friends.
- Socialize with others.
- Practice being intuitive every day.
- Be ethical with everyone.
- Be honest with yourself.
- Find a way to create value in challenging situations.

DON'T
- Try to be everybody's caretaker.
- Try to be Mother Teresa.
- Forget to recharge your batteries.

- Ignore your feelings.
- Try to control others.
- Let others bully or control you.
- Be too self-critical.
- Be a fault-finder.
- Be a people-pleaser all the time (Jane Fonda calls this the "disease to please").
- Expect immediate results—this is a process and a journey.

> **Twintuition Tip:**
> Psychic intelligence involves the emotions and the intellect.
>
> IQ + EQ = Psi-Q
>
> (Intelligence + emotional intelligence = psychic intelligence)

Now, before we move on, take a moment to determine your current level of psychic intelligence.

HOW HIGH IS YOUR PSI-Q?

To test yourself, answer yes or no to these questions. Scores at the end!

Answering yes to any one or more of the following questions is an indication that you may be psychically gifted in a particular area. As you read about the four Clairs in the following chapters you will learn what each of these abilities says about your own Psi-Q—and what you can do to increase all your psychic abilities.

1. Do you see shadowy figures at night?
2. When the phone rings, do you "know" who it is on the other end?
3. Do you have dreams that come true?
4. Are you a good judge of character?
5. Do you sometimes get "bad vibes" in crowded places?
6. Do you see auras or color fields around other people?

7. Are you easily affected by the moon or planetary changes?
8. Do you have an exceptionally good sense of direction?
9. Can you tell if someone is lying or being truthful?
10. Are you good at finding things that are hidden or lost?
11. Do you have a lot of coincidences occurring in your daily life?
12. Have you ever heard voices when no one is in the room with you?

Hint: If you're not sure of the answer, it's probably a no. If it was yes, you'd be aware of it.

Your score!
You answered yes to:

All 12 questions: You could be a super-psychic!
10–11: You are definitely psychically gifted.
7–9: You have many psychic talents.
4–6: You need to pay more attention to your inner guidance.
0–3: You may be shutting down or ignoring your natural psi abilities.

PART II

WHICH CLAIR ARE YOU?— THE FOUR KEYS TO MYSTICAL DOORWAYS

Some people are more verbal than visual; some are more intellectual than emotional—and vice versa. The same is true for psychic abilities. You may already have noticed this about yourself, and if you've wondered why you seem to "hear" information or advice from the higher realm or why you sometimes "feel" that something is very wrong—or very right—learning about the four Clairs will help you not only to understand why this is so but also to increase your Psi-Q in every area.

6

Stop! Look! Listen! Feel! Know!—Meet the Four Clairs

It is as dangerous to generalize about psychics as it is to generalize about all doctors or lawyers or writers or any other group of diversely talented individuals. Beyond that, any individual may be extremely capable or gifted in one area and sadly lacking in others. A brilliant surgeon who knows how to save lives on the operating table may be clueless about how to save a personal relationship. A brilliant director of costume dramas may have a tin ear when it comes to comedy. One of our clients was a top Fortune 500 CEO; she was a true genius in business but a bull in a china shop when it came to nurturing friendships. Her lack of empathy was a serious shortcoming that caused both her and those close to her a great deal of suffering.

Most people have a very limited concept of how psychics receive information. It actually comes in many different ways, and when it comes to psychic intelligence, you may score at the genius level in some areas and be average or below average in others. You can strengthen those areas where you're weak, but you'll always be more intuitively adept at some modes of "information gathering" than others. *"Clair"* is the French word for "clear," and each of the four Clairs—clairvoyance, clairaudience, claircognizance, and clairsentience—provides clarity through its own particular channel. All psychics use one or more of the Clairs to receive information.

No one way of receiving information is intrinsically better than any other, but knowing where you excel will help you to understand, for example, why you seem to hear the answers to your questions with your inner ear, or why you can predict outcomes before they occur. In addition, working to increase your abilities in those areas where you're less naturally gifted will increase the number of tools in your psychic toolbox.

Prophet or Pundit—The Difference between Rational and Intuitive Prediction

Pundits are generally recognized for their ability to forecast trends based upon a rational analysis of available data and an extrapolation of that data to determine the probability of future events. Prophets, on the other hand, predict events that are unexpected and cannot be anticipated through any rational or logical means. As psychics our Clairs are what allows us to make our predictions, but even pundits who forecast trends based on rational analysis will do better when they also use their intuition and allow their Clairs to assist them.

WHEN ONE SENSE IS LACKING

Pam is a lovely woman we know who has been blind since birth. As visual artists and clairvoyants who have always been quite obsessed with the world of art, design, and color, we find it almost impossible to imagine not having the gift of sight. When we asked Pam what it was like being blind, her response was eye-opening! Pam told us that blind people learn about life in a whole different way. Because they don't have a constant stream of information coming through their eyes into their brain, they rely on the senses of sound, touch, and smell to receive information.

She said that vision keeps people from thinking things through and feeling things completely. If she could see, she told us, she would not pay as much attention to the sounds around her. "I believe that each sound, smell, or texture has a spirit. I like to honor those spirits as much as I can. I don't know if I'd trade the blindness for sight. I know that I use my imagination much more than the sighted people I know. I hear a sound, and if I'm not sure what it is, I begin to imagine all the things it might be. That's pretty fun." Pam has a great deal to teach people who take their sight for granted.

We have several friends who were born deaf, and they are very intuitive as well. Being hearing-impaired has heightened their ability to sense in other ways and to rely more on their intuition. What surprises us most is that they don't need to have hearing to enjoy their lives. In fact, there are sounds—like snoring, for example—that they probably appreciate *not* hearing!

We have found that, in many cases, being hearing- or sight-impaired can increase a person's intuitive abilities, as that person is forced to rely more on his or her sixth sense to function in day-to-day life.

We have long joked that we are "full-service" psychics! We predict the future and talk to the dead. We are equally deft at crime-solving, medical intuition, and business counseling, and we are also gifted in all of the Clairs, although clairaudience is not one of our strongest modes of information-gathering. That said, however, each person—and that includes you—has a particular psychic strength or Clair, and each of the Clairs uses a unique kind of energy for achieving a higher level of clarity.

Chakras and Auras—Your Vibrational Energy Sources

We know that everything in the Universe has energy, that energy never dies, and that there are many different kinds of energy that vibrate at different frequencies. According to Eastern medicine, your body has seven cone-shaped energy centers called "chakras" located at different points along your spine. Each of the Clairs is associated with one of the chakras and utilizes the energy from that particular area to access information. The chakras also radiate our auras, the vibrational energy fields that surround all living things with rings of color. (See pages 40–42 for more information on auras.)

Here is a list of the seven chakras and their locations in the body, as well as the energies and colors with which they are associated:

> *First chakra*, also called the "root chakra," is located at the base of the spine and governs our survival instincts, financial issues, self-image, primary instincts (including sex drive), and the ability to function well on the physical plane. This chakra is associated with clairsentience and the color red.
>
> *Second chakra*, also called the "sacral chakra," is located in the lower abdomen, just below the navel, governs our creativity and emotional well-being, and is associated with the ability to take risks and defend oneself. This chakra is associated with clairsentience and with the color orange.
>
> *Third chakra*, also called the "will center," is located just below the breastbone, in the solar plexus. The third chakra governs the positive use of personal power, self-esteem, and the ability to manifest goals. It is associated with clairsentience and with the color yellow. In martial arts, the third chakra is thought to be the center of chi, the life force energy.
>
> *Fourth chakra* is located near the heart and governs love, forgiveness, compassion, and trust, as well as the release of suppressed emotions or trauma. It is associated with clairaudience and the color green.
>
> *Fifth chakra* is located in the base of the throat, just below the voice box, and governs the ability to communicate, as well as logic and reason, choice and will. It is connected with clairaudience and turquoise blue, the color of loving communication.

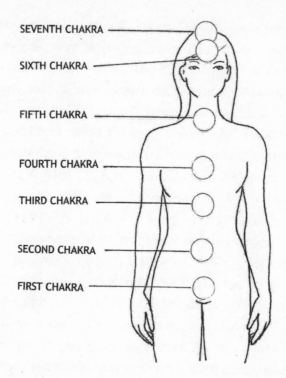

SEVENTH CHAKRA

SIXTH CHAKRA

FIFTH CHAKRA

FOURTH CHAKRA

THIRD CHAKRA

SECOND CHAKRA

FIRST CHAKRA

Sixth chakra, also called "the third eye," is located between the eyebrows and governs the ability to use one's intuition and see the bigger picture. It is associated with clairvoyance and the color indigo blue—which is why psychic children are often called "Indigo children."

Seventh chakra, also known as the "crown chakra," is located at the top of the head and governs intellectual thought, wisdom, and access to divine inspiration. It is associated with claircognizance and with the colors violet and white.

Using Our Clairs for Psychic Crime-Solving

The two of us have worked on many missing persons cases, and some high-profile murders, as psychic detectives. Doing this kind of work uses all four Clairs. Impressions can come in visually, or through feelings, sounds, or thoughts.

Whenever possible, we like going to the place where the crime was committed, or, if it's a missing person case, to the place they were last seen. So when the CBS show *The Insider* brought us in after Olivia Newton-John's boyfriend, Patrick McDermott, mysteriously vanished on a fishing boat off San Diego in June 2005, they took us to the wharf where McDermott had last been seen. On camera, we correctly predicted that he had faked his own death due to financial problems and was hiding in Mexico. In April 2010, McDermott was found by private investigators for *Dateline NBC* living near Puerto Vallarta, Mexico!

When going to the scene isn't possible, we can meditate on a photo of the missing person or the victim and receive impressions, such as flashes of a face, clothing, colors, smells, and emotions. We also use our automatic writing to describe the "who, what, when, and where" of everyone involved if we suspect a crime has been committed. (For more on automatic writing, see Chapter Fourteen.) Another tool to aid clairvoyance is printing out a map of the area where the person either lives or was last seen and circling the locations and names of cities to which your hands feel drawn. We also know of several psychics who have a sense of their hands "heating up" when they get close to a possible crime area on a map. If you want to try it, you'll find that, with practice, you'll figure out which techniques work best for you.

Linda once was able to help solve a rape case through her use of "channeled drawing"—a special type of clairvoyance that is perhaps less commonly used than automatic writing. While in her teens, Linda had a brief stint as a courtroom illustrator and was intrigued by murder cases. She had some of her courtroom drawings published in local Philadelphia papers. When our friend (we'll call her "Gia") was handcuffed and raped in her apartment by a man posing as a policeman, Linda suggested that Gia describe the man while she drew a picture of him using clairvoyance to get even more specific details. Together, they developed a likeness of the suspect and took it to the local police department. The police posted the drawing around the neighborhood, and the rapist was subsequently identified and arrested!

Just a year ago, as of this writing, we ourselves were being stalked. We were receiving up to eight death threats per day in the form of disturbing and violent e-mails, too vile to print here. It was an absolutely terrifying experience. We filed a report with the LAPD, and they referred us to the official celebrity stalker division of the Threat Management Unit.

We gave the detectives a detailed account of the situation and used our psychic profiling background to provide insights into who could possibly be stalking us. Working closely with the detectives over a period of months, we assisted the investigators in tracking him down. Our stalker turned out to be a client whom we had talked out of committing suicide years earlier. He was hacking into his neighbors' computer systems to send e-mail threats to us from all over his neighborhood.

We hope that you never find yourself in this kind of situation, but if you do, you, too, can use your Clairs to lead you to the guilty party.

Use Your Clairs to Enhance Your Life

Accessing one or more of the four Clairs is the way to receive information about your environment, people, or situations that might not be obvious to your rational, logical mind. You can call upon the Clairs in order to:

- Become happier
- Discover your life purpose
- Develop vibrant health
- Make more successful decisions
- Trust your innate guidance system
- Attract wealth and abundance
- Overcome your weaknesses
- Banish your fears and release emotional blocks
- Set healthy boundaries
- See danger coming
- Tune in to your higher guidance

- Bring forth greater wisdom
- Achieve your goals
- Find your most authentic self
- Create more meaningful relationships

In the following chapters we'll be describing each Clair in detail, providing specific exercises and techniques for determining which one works best for you; and we'll help you develop your abilities in that area so you are able to find the answers and solutions to your most difficult and challenging questions and problems.

WHICH CLAIR IS THIS? TAKE THE QUIZ!

Circle a, b, c, or d.

1. You have a good feeling about a new friend.
   a. Clairvoyance
   b. Clairaudience
   c. Claircognizance
   d. Clairsentience
2. You just know that your son, who lives out of state, had a car accident.
   a. Clairvoyance
   b. Clairaudience
   c. Claircognizance
   d. Clairsentience
3. You see a flock of geese flying in a V formation right before an important event occurs.
   a. Clairvoyance
   b. Clairaudience
   c. Claircognizance
   d. Clairsentience
4. You hear an inner voice warn you not to do something.
   a. Clairvoyance
   b. Clairaudience

   c. Claircognizance
   d. Clairsentience

5. You feel sad when you enter a certain restaurant.
   a. Clairvoyance
   b. Clairaudience
   c. Claircognizance
   d. Clairsentience

6. You have a gut feeling about a friend needing help.
   a. Clairvoyance
   b. Clairaudience
   c. Claircognizance
   d. Clairsentience

7. You hear a voice when you are driving telling you to turn right.
   a. Clairvoyance
   b. Clairaudience
   c. Claircognizance
   d. Clairsentience

8. You suddenly think to call an aunt and she tells you she just had emergency surgery.
   a. Clairvoyance
   b. Clairaudience
   c. Claircognizance
   d. Clairsentience

9. You get a mental picture of someone you haven't seen in years.
   a. Clairvoyance
   b. Clairaudience
   c. Claircognizance
   d. Clairsentience

10. You have a dream about twins, and a month later your daughter is pregnant with twins.
   a. Clairvoyance
   b. Clairaudience

c. Claircognizance
d. Clairsentience

Answers:
1. Clairsentience
2. Claircognizance
3. Clairvoyance
4. Clairaudience
5. Clairsentience
6. Clairsentience
7. Clairaudience
8. Claircognizance
9. Clairvoyance
10. Clairvoyance

Clairvoyance—Clear Seeing

Clairvoyance, or clear seeing, is also known as the gift of "psy-chic sight" or "second sight." Clairvoyant information can be either precognitive (i.e., directed forward to predict future events) or retrocognitive (also called "postcognitive," directed toward access-ing information about events that occurred in the past). Sometimes clairvoyant information comes in the form of literal images. Some-times it comes in the form of symbols. Omens and oracles are also an important part of clairvoyance. Throughout history there have been saints, seers, prophets, medicine men, and shamanic healers who have had clairvoyant experiences that defy the laws of common sense.

In what has been recorded as one of the first documented cases of clairvoyance, the Swedish scientist, politician, and mystic Eman-uel Swedenborg, while visiting friends in Gothenburg in 1756, had a vision of a terrible fire burning in Stockholm about three hundred miles away that was threatening his own home. Then, some hours later, he informed his hosts that he'd had another vision and that the fire had been extinguished. Two days later, the vision, which he had described in precise detail, was confirmed.

Among her many recorded visions, the famous Polish clairvoyant and healer Agnieszka Pilchowa foresaw the horrors of World War II when, in 1940, she said, "I see large countries filled with hatred and violence, confined with barbed wire. I see burning bodies, the smoke of hellish fires cover the sky. I see a swastika rolling eastwards. The two criminals of humanity will fight each other using hordes of their slaves and masses of their weapons. The ground will shake under their steps." Pilchowa died in 1944 in the Ravensbrück concentration camp.

SEEING IN PICTURES

With several best-selling books to her name and an HBO movie devoted to telling her story, Temple Grandin is now probably one of the best-known people in the world living with autism. While autism is a condition she would probably not have chosen and that no one should have to live with, it also gave her particular sensibilities and a remarkable intuitive gift.

Like many people with autism, Ms. Grandin is extremely sensitive to sound, which she once compared in a speech she gave at an annual conference of the Autism Society of America to "being tied to the rail and the train is coming."

But it is the way she thinks—by "seeing in pictures"—that has made her renowned in the field of animal behavior, because she has the very special ability to see the world through their eyes.

While we certainly don't in any way want to equate autism with psychic intelligence, we do—as people who experience the world differently from most—find it fascinating and enlightening that someone whom most would consider disabled can, at the same time, be gifted with such a heightened ability to see things intuitively.

How Clairvoyants See Things

Clairvoyants are very observant and attuned to their natural surroundings. We, for example, tend to notice various gradations of color in nature, the way sunlight glances off the side of a building, the changing shadows and subtle movements of the clouds. We notice the varieties of trees, gardens, rock formations, and flowers that most people would ignore or tune out. Indoors, we pay attention to design, colors and lighting, artwork and how it is displayed, and furniture placement. We are also great people-watchers. We love going to a park or a restaurant and observing the clothing, unique hairstyles, and quirky mannerisms or body language of the people around us.

Talent involving fashion design, painting, drawing, photography, filmmaking, and other visual arts also indicates that you are strong in the area of clairvoyance. If you have vivid dreams in Technicolor, or dreams of events that have not yet occurred (called "precognitive dreams"), you are clear seeing. Intuitive healers, otherwise known as "medical intuitives," can sometimes develop the ability to see into the body of the person they are working on. Certain organs will glow in a particular color or appear to the healer visually.

Clairvoyant psychics and mediums often see figures and events in their mind's eye, almost like a movie being projected onto a small screen. Both of us have experienced this phenomenon.

We believe that our own clairvoyant abilities are linked to our abilities as artists. Not only have we been artists and painters our entire lives, but both of us have also had experience teaching art to grades kindergarten through college. Terry even taught art to blind children in Philadelphia. We have no doubt that our visual talents and the fact that we constantly exercised our creative skills greatly heightened our sense of clairvoyance. Terry will literally visualize her paintings before she even picks up a brush, as though the images had been given to her by the spirit world.

We naturally think in colors, pictures, and symbols, and we believe that artists, musicians, and writers, who practice seeing and listening all day long, every day, tend to be more intuitive than others because, as we've said, they are using the creative powers of their right brain. When we were sixteen we doubled as the lead in a play for our French class (like the Olsen twins on *Full House*). We shared the role of the Little Prince in *Le Petit Prince* wearing identical navy pantsuits with red trim. The line we liked most in the play was *"L'essential est invisible pour les yeux"* ("What is essential is invisible to the eyes").

At the time, we had no idea that we would one day become leading experts on the invisible world! In retrospect, we can see that this was an omen for us—a sign of what our future would hold.

If you close your eyes and call up from memory the mental image of a person or place you know extremely well, you will undoubtedly see a clear picture in your mind of whatever it is you've chosen. That's the kind of clear picture we get when we're receiving clairvoyant information, except that the image or visual impression does not come from memory and it arrives uninvited, without our having consciously called it up—and very often when we are doing something entirely different.

Especially while you are still honing your skills, the edges of the picture you see may not always be sharp. Sometimes things are blurry, overlapping, or only partly formed. Don't worry about it. Just keep practicing and refining your ability.

CLAIRVOYANCE TO THE RESCUE

On one segment of his television program, Dr. Mehmet Oz interviewed Officer Bell, a police officer who was among the last wave of rescue workers in New Orleans following Hurricane Katrina.

Two weeks after the hurricane Officer Bell was revisiting a house that had already been checked several times before by rescue workers looking for survivors, and sealed up.

Nevertheless, Bell had a strong clairvoyant sense that someone was still alive inside and issued an order to break in. Sure enough, there was a man inside, alive but barely breathing, and Bell was able to get him out just in time. The police had been told they weren't authorized to enter homes unless they were absolutely certain someone was inside. While Bell had no proof, he trusted his intuitive vision and was compelled to break down the security door immediately.

"Intuition must be an important part of your line of work if you are willing to go against what you were told to do because you felt so strongly about it," said Dr. Oz. "Yes, sir, yes, it is," Bell replied.

Tarot Cards Can Enhance Clairvoyance

One psychic client of ours uses tarot cards to increase clairvoyance with relation to the person she's reading. The tarot deck, which is generally used to aid divination or foreseeing the future, commonly has seventy-eight cards with four suits corresponding to the suits of conventional playing cards. Each of these suits has ten numbered cards and four face cards for a total of fourteen in each suit. In addition, there are twenty-one illustrated trump cards, and a single card known as "the Fool." The trump cards are the ones most of us think of when we think of tarot—the High Priestess, the Hanged Man, the Devil, the Magician, and so on. Each of the pictorial symbols also has a particular meaning attached to it, and sometimes multiple meanings depending on the colors, numbers, and images. The High Priestess, for example, represents intuitive wisdom, and the Hanged Man represents the need to change. The person reading the tarot shuffles the cards and then asks the subject for whom he is reading to cut the deck. The reader lays out the cards in a particular pattern and uses the numbers and images that turn up to trigger intuitive impressions. While each card has a specific assigned meaning, looking at the images can also be a catalyst for the flow of clairvoyant information in much the same way automatic writing works for us. In other words, without knowing the assigned meaning of a particular card, for people who are clairvoyant the picture itself can inspire the occurrence of intuitive thoughts about the person for whom they are reading.

Exercises to Strengthen Your Clairvoyance

If you feel drawn to this visual kind of "knowing," here are a few exercises you can do to strengthen your abilities and learn how to interpret the pictures you receive. By practicing these skills you'll be able to "see around corners" and envision a new reality for yourself.

Practice "Seeing" with Your Third Eye

Choose a close friend or relative. Now close your eyes, focus your mind, and try to see with your inner eye where that person is at that very moment, what they are doing, and what they're wearing. What room are they in? What does the furniture look like? Notice as many details as you can. When your mental picture is as clear as you can make it, open your eyes, note the date and time, and record what you saw in your journal. Then call the person and see how close your mental image came to reality. This exercise is fun, especially if the other person is far away. You'll be surprised at how accurate you can be!

Color Your Memories

Using colored pencils, crayons, or markers, draw the house you grew up in. Using your imagination, color each room, each window, and the garden out front. Were there dogs, cats, deer, or other animals? Do you recall gardens or trees around your house? Include as much color as possible. What color would you make the sky? Try not to be too realistic. This exercise is about developing your creative sense. Try not to censor yourself or second-guess the colors you choose. Allow your imagination free play and just pick up whatever color inspires you, whether it's realistic or not. Working with color is a way to strengthen clairvoyance because your choices tend to reflect your emotions. You may, for example, be drawn to light colors to draw happy memories. Dark colors may indicate some kind of fear or anger associated with the picture you are drawing. When you feel that your drawing is finished, think about what it reminds you of. Do you know why you chose those particular colors? What do the colors you chose have to tell you about the feelings you associate with the house? Record what you feel and remember in your journal.

Make a Collage

Over the past thirty years, Linda has used collage as a basis for much of her artwork. The word "collage" is taken from the French verb *"coller,"* which means "to paste or glue." The basic process of collage is pasting or gluing paper to paper, or paper to board.

Linda collects vintage magazines, preferably from the fifties and sixties, as well as books with photos, and cuts out images that appeal to her, that have a personal symbolism, and that resonate emotionally.

Sometimes she sits on the floor with magazines and clippings all around her and just cuts and pastes images on paper, juxtaposing unusual combinations of images or text without really thinking about why she's choosing them or why she's arranging them in that particular way. She doesn't plan in advance what she's going to do. She's just giving free rein to her artistic instincts and often, the layered images she comes up with turn out to evoke a strong emotional response.

Gather a selection of old magazines, photos, and other images. Cut the images into whatever shapes strike your fancy, arrange them on a piece of paper or cardboard, and glue them into a pattern that appeals to you. What is fun is seeing how an image takes on a whole new meaning when it is placed next to a totally unrelated image or phrase. The results are often delightfully humorous. Doing collage work can also help to trigger imaginative associations and jump-start your intuition. Collage is a great way to "rearrange reality" and open yourself up to the idea of "seeing" things in a whole new light.

Try Scrapbooking

Scrapbooking is a form of collage popularly used to preserve all kinds of mementos. You can buy beautiful scrapbooking papers and kits at craft stores. Use old postcards, maps, postage stamps, seashells, ribbons, stickers, rubber stamps, or anything else that appeals to you, and "bedazzle" your pages with sparkles and rhinestones that can be purchased inexpensively in small plastic packets. Shop at thrift stores and resale shops for old lace and vintage cards, sheet music, or fabrics. Scrapbooking doesn't have to cost a lot. Just make sure you have plenty of room and a variety of materials to work with. The idea, as with collage, is to spontaneously juxtapose disparate objects and images as they strike you so that you begin to see the unusual in the otherwise mundane.

Do Something Different—Or Do It Differently

The brain, as we've said, thrives on diversity and novelty. So doing something that is visually new and different will help to open pathways that stimulate clairvoyance.

Spend an afternoon in a museum. Abstract paintings beg you to use your visual imagination, while classical portraits may inspire you to imagine the life of the sitter or trigger memories of one of your own past lives.

As a child, did your parents take you to the zoo? What was your favorite animal, and how did that animal make you feel? We always loved the zebras with their graphic stripes. Take a trip to the zoo and try to imagine which animal you would like to be. Reread an old book and really try to visualize the characters and their surroundings. Rewatch an old movie that made a strong emotional impression on you and pay attention to details you may have missed before. See if those old feelings begin to surface and, if so, reexamine them.

Try experimenting with a new makeup color palette, or put together an outfit using colors and styles you don't normally wear. Go to a vintage store and buy some brightly colored Fiestaware or china that is different from what you have at home, and create a new table setting. Take a trip to the beach and collect pebbles and shells and glue them to a picture frame, or make a shell mosaic. Whenever our father, a professional painter, felt stuck or had artist's block with a painting, he would go to a junkyard and collect random metal or wooden objects that he would then use to make very creative abstract collages. Doing that would usually stimulate his creativity so that he could return to his painting with a fresh eye.

Try painting one wall of your living room or bedroom a bright accent color that is a bit out of your comfort zone. Take a risk—you can always paint over it. We once painted an entire living room wall bright chartreuse! It really made us feel alive, and afterward we went on a very creative streak and made quite a lot of art as a result. If you make quilts or sew, you can try gathering swatches of odd colorful vintage fabrics. Leaf through a craft book to get ideas for a wall hanging, quilt, or throw pillows for the sofa. When we want a visual change, Linda sews bold-patterned pillows for the couch that change the whole feeling of the room.

Design an aquarium with some exotic fish. If you are a guy, you may want to build a simple piece of furniture. Make your own movie on your computer. There are programs that can help you do this fairly inexpensively, and the result is often quite astonishing. Design your own website or blog. You can get very creative with the colors, images, photos, and fonts, as well as the writing.

HOW CLAIRVOYANT ARE YOU? TAKE THE QUIZ!

Answer yes or no to the following questions:

1. Do you find yourself drawn to the visual arts?
2. Do you like to draw, paint, or design things?
3. Do you love clothing and fashion?
4. Do you have vividly dramatic dreams that are often in Technicolor?
5. Do you get images or "flashes" of future events that come true?
6. Can you visualize someone without having met him or her?
7. Do you get spontaneous visual impressions in the course of the day that have nothing to do with what you were consciously thinking about at the time?
8. Do you notice flowers, trees, and nature in detail?
9. Are you aware of auras or color fields surrounding people?
10. Are you able to "X-ray" a person or pet to see where they may have an illness?

If you answered yes to five or more of these questions, you are definitely clairvoyant. Doing the exercises in this chapter will help you to develop your talent even more. But don't stop there! Go on to read the chapters that follow. You may already be gifted in more than one Clair, and you can always improve upon your abilities even in those that may not be your strongest.

Remember—there's no one way that's better than others to receive psychic information, but the more skills you have at your disposal, the greater your intuitive versatility will be.

8

Clairaudience—Clear Hearing

Do you hear subtle messages that others do not—quiet whispers, bells ringing, music, footsteps in the night, voices that seem to come from another dimension? Clairaudience is a kind of inner or supernormal hearing—the ability to hear things outside the range of normal perception—and is associated with the fifth chakra, the throat center. Many musicians and writers have cited it as the inspiration for their works.

Since ancient times, prophets, priests, saints, and mystics have been guided by clairaudient voices, usually interpreted as the voice of God, angels, spirit guides, or some other nonphysical being or divine essence. The ancient Greeks believed spirit beings known as "daimons" acted as intermediaries sent by the deities to whisper guidance in the ears of men, and the Bible contains many stories in which God sends messages through an intermediary to prophets and kings, which could be interpreted as instances of clairaudience.

Old Testament prophets, including Moses, Samuel, Jacob, Ezekiel, and Elijah, were often instructed by angelic voices to convey messages—often in the nature of warnings to kings.

In the New Testament, clairaudient messages brought good news more often than bad. For example, on the occasion of Jesus's baptism in the wilderness, both he and John the Baptist heard God say, "Thou art my beloved Son; in thee I am well pleased" (Luke 3:22).

Throughout history men and women have used their clairaudient gifts. Joan of Arc, at an early age, not only saw visions but also heard the voices of angels, which inspired her courageous mission to lead the French army to several important victories during the Hundred Years' War.

In some traditional Tibetan and Native Indian cultures, children were taught from an early age to listen to the subtle sounds of nature because people relied on this attunement and intense way of listening as powerful survival tools.

In modern times, however, we've come to doubt our clairaudient powers because we associate people's talking to themselves or "hearing voices" with signs of mental illness. (And those guys wandering around the grocery store talking into an invisible phone headset do seem absolutely bonkers.)

When you are truly receiving a message that comes from a higher, more intuitive level of hearing, however, it will probably seem more like a sudden insight than an extraterrestrial command. And it will never suggest anything that might put you or anyone else in danger. It may occur either as the actual perception of sound, such as someone whispering in your ear, or as a thought, as if you were silently talking to yourself. We all have these internal mental dialogues from time to time, but clairaudient messages are distinguished by the fact that they pop into your head uninvited, and often when you're in the midst of thinking about something entirely different.

You may hear ringing in your ears for no apparent reason, or your name being whispered when no one is home but you. Sometimes you'll hear a voice as if it were coming from another room. We know one clairaudient person who hears many spirit voices at once, like a group conversation. The trick for her is sorting out who is saying what! She sometimes has to say, "Okay, you guys—one at a time!" Or you might hear a loud swishing sound, almost like ocean waves, or feel as if your ears are clogging up with water. We very often feel that our ears are stuffy. If you have a similar sensation, it might be a sign that your psychic hearing is being calibrated or attuned to higher frequencies of sound. You may be extremely sensitive to any kind of sound, from loud rock music to barking dogs, and capable of hearing other people's conversations across an entire room. Sometimes we hear voices chanting when we are alone in our apartment. Some people hear birds chirping, metal clanging, and even orchestral melodies.

Very psychic people can hear the voices of angels and spirit guides, especially at crucial moments when they need protection or guidance. The messages are often very simple and loving. A friend of ours told us that she becomes clairaudient only in situations of extreme stress. When that happens, she knows that she needs to pay attention. The two of us often hear angels calling our names, and once, when we were going through an especially difficult illness, we both heard the same angelic voice say, "Don't worry, dear ones, everything will be fine. Be so confident." And it was fine! We can always ask for guidance, but it also seems to come to us unsolicited when we truly need it. If the same is true for you, you are probably gifted in the area of clairaudience.

Perhaps the most dramatic example of our receiving a clairaudient message occurred when we were home one day and both heard a voice say, "Olivia needs help." We instantly thought of our neighbor, Olivia, and ran next door to find her struggling to breathe. We called 911 and stayed with her, praying softly, until the paramedics arrived just in time to save her life. She had taken an herb to which she had an allergic reaction and went into anaphylactic shock. She later told us from her hospital bed that she had been unable to speak or call for help. If we hadn't "heard" that angelic cry for help, she wouldn't be with us today.

Exercises to Increase Your Clairaudience

Some people seem to hear every little sound, no matter how soft or how far away it is. This can be extremely annoying if it's the sound of someone's radio playing halfway down the block. But if you're try-ing to develop your clairaudience, doing exercises that sharpen your hearing will also improve your ability to receive psychic messages that come from the world of spirit. Here are a few suggestions for how you can begin to increase your clairaudient awareness. Doing these simple exercises over time will help to turn up the volume in your inner ear.

Listen Up! A Meditation to Open Clairaudience

Sit in a comfortable position and take several deep breaths.

Imagine your hearing being cleared by spinning balls of white light.

Take another deep breath and imagine that all your painful mem-ories of hurtful words are dissolving and being released.

We all have guardian angels (see Chapter Eleven). Ask yours to help you release the doubt or fear that may be blocking your inner hearing.

You may notice an increase in your clairaudience fairly soon after doing this meditation. Repeat it daily until you do. Don't try to cen-sor or dismiss what comes to you. Try not to have any preconceived notions of what you'll receive. The guidance you receive may not be what you expected or what you wanted to hear!

How Many Instruments Can You Hear?

Plug into your iPod or put on a CD and listen to one of your favorite pieces of music. See how many individual instruments or voices you can distinguish. Can you pick out the guitar? The bass? The piano? Backup singers? Now, gradually turn down the sound and see how long you continue to hear it. You can hone this skill by first deciding that you'll listen just to the piano or the violins or the trombone. Then try to hear two at once, and so on, until you are able to hear multiple distinct instruments at once.

Try Tuning In to What You Normally Tune Out

Sounds are all around us all the time; it's just that we spend most of our life trying to tune them out. Try to tune in for a change. Take a walk outdoors, in the park or on a busy street, and notice how many sounds you usually tune out—a plane flying overhead, the different calls that birds make, and a train whistle, car horns, truck tires, a baby crying. Or go to a busy restaurant and eavesdrop on the conversations around you. How many individual voices can you pick out? Can you follow the conversation even when people are talking over one another? Isn't it fun?

Walk Away from the Sound

When you're outside, focus on a loud noise in a particular location. It could be music coming from a public place or the sound of a waterfall or an engine. Now walk away from the source of the sound and see how long you can continue to hear it. As we've said, sharpening your hearing will help to increase your clairaudience. What you're doing in this and the other exercises in this chapter is learning to really listen—something many of us don't do so well in the course of daily life.

HOW CLAIRAUDIENT ARE YOU? TAKE THE QUIZ!

Answer yes or no to the following questions:

1. Are you highly sensitive to noises or loud music?
2. Do you often have ringing in your ears?
3. Do you hear sounds that others don't seem to hear?
4. Do you sometimes hear your name called when there is no one in the room with you?
5. Are you annoyed by loud sounds like barking dogs or crying babies?
6. Do you avoid rock concerts and clubs with loud music?
7. Do you ever have a "swishing" sound in your ears?

8. Do you prefer to listen to good music rather than watching TV?
9. Do you hear random words or whispers during the day?
10. Can you detect what other people are saying, even if they are across the room?

If you answered yes to five or more of these questions, clairaudience may be your strongest Clair. Keep on practicing, and read on to discover and nurture the other Clairs as well.

9

Claircognizance—Clear Knowing

C laircognizance is the strongest Clair for the two of us, although, as we've said, we do use all the others as well. Claircognizance comes in like a thought, an idea, a knowing; it is associated with the seventh chakra, located at the top of the head. People who are claircognizant tend to be logical and extremely analytical. They are classic know-it-alls who always seem to have an answer for everything. We were always very cerebral as kids, and we obsessively analyze everything. Claircognizants tend to be workaholics, good at problem-solving, and very inventive by nature. They are good at abstract thinking and have great organizational skills. In fact many claircogs, like us, are compulsive thinkers. We have to consciously release the need to analyze everything. Strategizing and analyzing are not always the most efficient ways to solve a problem. Analyzing is a bit like worrying—it doesn't always lead to the best result, and it tends to block intuition.

Instead of coming through as a vision or a voice, claircognizant messages are more like thoughts that suddenly pop into your head. Unlike your normal, everyday thoughts, they seem to come out of the blue and usually have no relation to whatever you may be consciously thinking about at the time. For example, you may be focusing on a Lifetime movie, when suddenly your neighbor's dog pops into your mind. The next day you might then hear that the dog had been rushed to the vet just at the time when the thought occurred. Or, out of nowhere, you think of a particular film star and then turn on the television to hear that he or she has just done something newsworthy.

Pay attention to novel ideas that come to you like a flash of inspiration, what we call "Aha! lightbulb moments." You may have heard that you should trust the very first thought that comes into your mind, because it usually turns out to be the most accurate. That is claircognizance. People tend to get into trouble when they start second-guessing themselves, thinking, "But what if...," or "But maybe I should..." Try not to overanalyze your gut instinct. Claircognizant "knowing" comes from a deeply instinctive place.

For example, one day years ago we were driving in New Jersey with Terry's then-boyfriend, Steve. Suddenly, Steve veered onto the shoulder of the road and cried, "Earthquake—San Francisco!" We later learned that this was the exact moment when the San Francisco earthquake of 1988 had occurred! Steve was a visual artist and a gifted claircognizant or "knower."

As another example, we were taking a walk one day in 2008 when Linda suddenly stopped and blurted out "Train crash!" Terry's watch said 4:20 p.m. When we returned home we saw on the news that a Metrolink commuter train had crashed head-on into a Union Pacific freight train, killing twenty-five people and injuring 135. The disaster—the second-worst railway accident in U.S. history—had occurred in nearby Chatsworth (about twenty minutes from our home) just minutes *after* Linda shouted it, at exactly 4:23 p.m. Linda had received the information like a broadcasting signal to her brain just moments before the disaster happened.

An article published in the London *Evening Standard* in 2007 quotes Professor Dick Bierman, a psychologist at the University of Amsterdam, who has conducted paranormal experiments using brain scans, as stating, "We're satisfied that people can sense the future before it happens." And Professor Brian Josephson, a Nobel

Prize—winning physicist from Cambridge University, concurred: "So far, the evidence seems compelling. What seems to be happening is that information is coming from the future. In fact, it's not clear in physics why you can't see the future. In physics, you certainly cannot completely rule out this effect." And other scientific experiments have also shown that people can see or sense future events before they occur.

In an experiment reported in the London *Evening Standard,* Dr. Dean Radin hooked up volunteers to a kind of lie detector that measured an electric current moving across the surface of the skin that changes when someone reacts to an event like seeing a violent picture or video. He then showed the volunteers images that were sexually explicit, violent, or soothing and noticed that the current changed moments *before* they saw the violent images with a regularity that could not be explained simply as coincidence or chance. They reacted to what *was going to appear on the screen* seconds before it actually did. In effect, the experiment showed that people can and do "know" things before they occur.

You may not know that you are having a claircognizant thought until the event occurs and you realize that you "knew it" before it happened. When it does, use that experience to validate and encourage your trust in your abilities.

Over time, we have developed the ability to differentiate the thoughts we generate with our conscious mind from those that are coming to us from the world of spirit, and the more you become aware of and develop your own claircognizance, the better you will be at doing that, too.

When you have a claircognizant thought, your conscious mind is simply the observer, not the creator of the information it receives. Very often, claircognizant thoughts come as a type of warning, and because they seem to come "out of left field," we tend to ignore them or brush them aside. Don't do that! Those thoughts and impressions that something important may be happening to which you should be paying attention could be giving you the heads-up that will either save your life or change it dramatically for the better.

A client told us about how his claircognizance had saved his life not once but three times! All three times he was in his car. The first time, he had a strange sense that he needed to stay at a stoplight even though it had turned green. People were honking their car horns, but he didn't budge. Within seconds, a fully loaded dump truck ran the red light and flew past just in front of him. Had he gone forward when the light changed, the truck would have hit him. The second time, the same thing happened, but this time it was an eighteen-wheeler! And the third time it was a school bus full of children. On each occasion his intuition saved his life.

We should point out here, however, that repetitive negative thoughts or unfounded fears are *not* claircognizance. If you have these kinds of thoughts and fears, they are being self-generated, as are any thoughts you might have of doing something harmful to yourself or another person. As we've said before, angelic or higher messages will *never* instruct you to hurt yourself or someone else. They can, however, warn you of a danger to come.

Twintuition Tip:
You can't change another person's path, even if you see the danger signs ahead.

Many people tell us that they've had a "premonition" of some unfortunate or dangerous event that didn't seem to make any sense until the event actually occurred. And afterward, they usually felt guilty for not having done anything to stop it. If that's ever happened to you, we want to assure you that there was probably nothing you could have done to change that particular sequence of events, or to prevent another person's karmic path from unfolding. As an example of this, during a private phone session we had with a woman not so long ago, Terry kept writing "car accident, two months ago" and the name "Victoria." When she asked if this was meaningful, the caller became extremely emotional and said that her close neighbor Victoria had been killed by a car two months earlier on her way to a New Year's Eve party. Even more amazing, she told us that she'd had a vision of her neighbor's impending death and implored her not to go to the party. She'd described her vision to Victoria in detail, even telling her who would be responsible for the accident and where it would occur. Sadly, Victoria ignored her friend's warning and lost her life. Terry then channeled this message from Victoria in her automatic writing: "I should have listened to you. You were right. I didn't want to believe you."

ISHTAR

Thoughts and impressions often pop into our minds when we are relaxed and preoccupied with everyday activities. Back in 2002, we were meeting in a restaurant with some producers who brought along Dr. Gary Schwartz. A friendly bearded man in his fifties, Dr. Schwartz is the author of *The Living Energy Universe* and *The Afterlife Experiments* and a noted researcher in the field of paranormal phenomena.

Dr. Schwartz was asking us about our work while we perused the menu when suddenly, out of nowhere, Linda said, "What is your connection to *Ishtar*?" Gary looked like he had been hit by a stun gun! He froze for about ten seconds. "I can't believe you would ask me that! *Ishtar* is my absolute favorite movie of all time! I really love that film. That really left me speechless!" (Well, this in itself is interesting since *Ishtar* is considered one of the most expensive Hollywood flops of all time, but anyway...) Linda then told Gary that *Ishtar* was also the name of one of his spirit guides.

While not everyone would consider this normal dinner conversation, we knew that Gary, because of his interest in all things psychic, would be receptive to receiving this information.

Exercises for Increasing Claircognizance

Just by having a strong intention to open up your claircognizance, you will become more highly aware of your thoughts and surroundings and will begin to notice claircognizant thoughts you might have ignored in the past. Here are a few exercises you can use to get started. You will be surprised at the information you are able to receive with just a little practice.

Open Your Crown Chakra

To access the energy center associated with claircognizance, sit quietly, consciously clear your mind, and try to visualize your crown chakra at the top of your head opening like a funnel or a lotus flower so that the information you receive can flow freely. The crown chakra, you will remember, governs intellectual thought, wisdom, and access to divine inspiration.

Ask for What You Need

Find a quiet place, focus your mind, and ask your angels and guides for any messages that are important for you to know. (For more on how to call upon angels and spirit guides, see Chapter Eleven.) Trust and accept that the thoughts you receive are true and write them in your journal so that you can validate them later.

Fictionary

Mothers often have a kind of sixth sense that lets them know when their children aren't telling the truth, but claircognizant people tend to know immediately whenever *anyone* is lying to them.

When we were young, we used to love playing the game "Fictionary." It is especially fun with a lot of people playing, but it can work with just two or three friends. One person picks an obscure word from the dictionary and writes down the definition (the sillier-sounding words are the best). When the word is read aloud, the other players make up a clever definition for the word and write it on a piece of paper. Everyone puts their definitions in a bowl, and the person with the dictionary (the "Picker") reads them all aloud, being sure to include the actual definition in the mix. People then vote for what they think is the real definition of the word. The definitions can be very funny, and the game will not only expand your vocabulary but also help you to become more intuitive about knowing whether or not people are telling the truth.

To Tell the Truth

Invite a bunch of friends over for a "Liar's Party." Everyone gathers around and, one by one, each person makes a statement or describes an event in two or three sentences while the others guess whether he or she is telling the truth. Listen closely and watch the storyteller's expression, and you will quickly get better at knowing instinctively when someone is lying.

HOW CLAIRCOGNIZANT ARE YOU? TAKE THE QUIZ!

Answer yes or no to the following questions:

1. Do you know when someone is lying to you?
2. Do you somehow just *know* when someone is trying to cheat you?
3. Do you receive inspired ideas that seem to come from nowhere?
4. Have you ever been positive that you shouldn't do something, even though everyone else thinks it's a great idea?
5. Have you thought about a particular person or event for no reason and then had it pop up in the news or on television the very next day?
6. Did you ever have a thought while in the shower, while doing laundry, or while doing some other mundane task, that later came to fruition?
7. Have you ever met someone and immediately had the thought that he or she would make a good partner for you?

8. Do you sometimes know intuitively that a person, a place, or a particular activity will be dangerous for you, only to learn later that you were correct?

If you answered yes to at least half these questions, you are definitely claircognizant. Practice the exercises in this chapter and learn to trust what you "know." But don't stop yet. Keep reading to find out if you're also clairsentient, and how to increase those "clear feelings."

10

Clairsentience—Clear Feeling

Clairsentience differs from claircognizance in the sense that the latter is a more intellectual type of knowing, while the former occurs as a strong physical or emotional reaction in the body.

Clairsentients often walk into a house and immediately sense that the energy is positive or negative. What they are picking up on may be the energy of people who have been there, not the house itself. People who have visited Gettysburg or other famous battlegrounds have reported feeling fear, anger, or pain, which is the emotional energy of the soldiers who died there. Clairsentients may also feel the fear of other patients in a dentist's office or the reverence of former worshippers in a church or cathedral. Again, they are feeling the lingering energy of those who have been in that particular space.

Clairsentients are "empaths" or "sensitives," who absorb the energy or vibrations of others like a sponge, often unconsciously, because they instinctively "feel your pain." They are also very sensitive to the pain and emotions of strangers, so they may be exceedingly uncomfortable in crowds at shopping malls or at sold-out arenas during sporting events. They may even sense the suffering of disaster victims, even if the event occurs miles away. And clairsentients are able to sense the emotions of others just from holding an object that belongs to them. (In Chapter Fifteen we talk about how you can practice doing this yourself.)

Interestingly, we've also found that clairsentients tend to be particularly sensitive to fluorescent lighting. They are more likely than most people to get headaches, feel dizzy or tired, and become anxious when exposed to this kind of light. While we aren't certain why so many clairsentients respond this way, we presume it's because they have a heightened sensitivity to certain kinds of light waves.

Because they are so sensitive, it is particularly important for clairsentients to protect themselves from the negativity of others. The two of us had to learn to protect ourselves from being affected by the toxic energy of other people so that we would not become physically and emotionally drained. We have felt stabbing pains in our back or stomach around very disturbed people. If you are feeling very uncomfortable, it is wise to remove yourself from the situation. Take a walk outside if you can. Find a quiet place to sit, and imagine the negative energy like a dark shape that moves down your legs and through the soles of your feet, leaving your body and going into the earth.

There are many different degrees of clairsentience, ranging from "feeling" other people's pain or illness in your own body, which is medical intuition, to feeling other people's emotions. Clairsentients may, for example, feel a tightening in the chest or a pain in some specific part of their body that lets them know another person is suffering from a particular illness. Very often, we've both been doubled over with abdominal pain when we're doing a reading for someone who is holding on to some emotional pain he or she desperately needs to let go. In effect, we can feel that person's pain or anger even when he or she isn't willing or able to acknowledge it.

We once received an e-mail from someone who told us:

I gave my sister a hug and within a few minutes I had muscle spasms in my upper back, and a headache. I was walking away when I realized I had not felt either of those symptoms before encountering her. So I walked back to my sister and told her, "You have muscle pain in your upper back and a throbbing headache on both sides of your head. Would you like some aspirin?" She looked absolutely amazed and asked, "How did you know that?"

Clairsentients often literally feel pain in the same part of their body as the person they are with, especially if they have a close connection with that person.

If you are clairsentient, you may also experience moments when you are suddenly overcome by a wave of emotion, such as sadness, or anxiety that has no logical cause. What's happening then is that you're picking up these emotions from other people—particularly people who are depressed—in your environment. If you ever get a strong feeling to avoid a certain person or situation, trust that feeling, even if it doesn't make sense right away. Heed that inner feeling. You may also get a bad "vibe" when you meet someone for the first time, and this, too, is clairsentience. Trust that gut feeling! Sometimes it may actually come in the form of a tummy ache or a pain in the neck, because those who are clairsentient may feel pain in their neck, back, or stomach or even feel faint when they are with someone who is especially negative. By the same token, they may feel a sense of safety, comfort, or well-being around someone who is very spiritual. For that very reason clairsentients should try to surround themselves with as many upbeat, happy, and confident people as possible.

THE BIG UNEASY—GETTING A "BAD FEELING"

We often hear from people who tell us chilling stories about the "bad feelings" they had about another person being in danger. When they recount these experiences, we pay attention to the language they use. Clear-seeing people will say, "I saw a picture of him lying dead by the side of the road," or "I had a dream that his car was going to crash into a bridge." Clear-feeling people tell us: "I had a terrible queasy feeling in the pit of my stomach that something bad was going to happen if she got in that car," or "My heart started beating so fast that I felt as if I were going to faint." One woman we met at a friend's Thanksgiving dinner (we'll call her "Cassie") told us a startling story about something horrible that had happened to her boss, Don, just a few days earlier.

Don was a lawyer and an experienced pilot, and Cassie was clearly still in shock as she recounted the story of the overwhelmingly eerie feeling she'd had about a flight he was about to take, even though he had flown countless times before without incident. She had confided her fears to some of her coworkers who, amazingly, had shared her sense of foreboding about their boss's taking this trip. They banded together and pleaded with him to reconsider flying that night. It was snowing, and the weather forecast was not good. Don, however, just laughed off their fears, saying that he wasn't worried; he'd flown in snowstorms before and had never had a problem. Still, Cassie couldn't shake off her heavy feeling of dread as she said good-bye to her boss that evening. He waved to everyone as he left, calling out, "See you tomorrow. Hold down the fort. Don't worry about me."

Later that night, Cassie's husband, a firefighter, just happened to be listening to his ham radio when he heard the emergency call: "Plane down. Cessna 172 Skyhawk. No survivors."

When he told her about it, Cassie's heart sank. She knew immediately that her premonition had come true. Don's plane had crashed in the storm shortly after takeoff and he was killed instantly. Cassie had trusted her clairsentience, but her boss had dismissed it. This is a perfect example of why we all need to use our psychic intelligence. It can make the difference between life and death.

Reiki—Healing through Touch

Reiki (pronounced ray-kee) is an ancient healing technique that sometimes opens up the practitioner to becoming more clairsentient and "feeling" another person's source of pain. The word "Reiki" comes from two Japanese words, *"rei"* meaning "universal" and *"ki"* (the equivalent of "chi" in Chinese) meaning "life force." The Reiki practitioner places his hands on the person with a healing intention. His energy will then go wherever it is most needed, as Reiki energy has its own innate intelligence. The practitioner need not consciously "direct" the energy. Staying calm and focused is all that is required for the most beneficial results. After treatment, the subject or patient will be completely relaxed, with a heightened sense of peace and well-being. We have been practicing Reiki for fifteen years, and, although it is not part of the process, we often chant at the same time to increase the healing power.

Many years ago, Linda had a job supervisor named Kimberly who was very involved in cat rescue work. To call her a cat fanatic would be a huge understatement—she had seventeen cats in her small apartment near the beach! One day Kimberly arrived at work with a small basket holding three tiny newborn kittens. Linda noticed that one of the kittens wasn't moving at all, and Kimberly explained it was the "runt of the litter" and would probably die in a short time, as most do. Instinctively, Linda put her hands on the kitten and began to chant softly, silently asking for angelic support. Within minutes the kitten was jumping around, clawing the side of the basket, and trying to get out! Kimberly said she had never seen anything like it in a lifetime of rescuing kittens, and she later told Linda that the so-called runt had become the strongest of the litter.

Anyone can learn this technique, and there are holistic healing centers all over the country that offer classes. We often recommend that our clients and students study Reiki healing to increase clairsentience.

Exercises for Increasing Your Clairsentience

The Empty Chair

Two teachers from Arthur Findlay College in Stansted, England, taught us this exercise to increase our clairsentience. To try it you will need a group of several people—including you—seated in a room together. Leave one seat empty. You then leave the room while one of the remaining people gets up and sits in the empty chair. When that person returns to his original seat, someone needs to call you back into the room. Sit in the empty chair and see if you can feel the energy of the person who has just gotten up. Are you feeling calm? Nervous? Hot? Cold? Relaxed or angry? See if you can identify the person who had been sitting there.

When we tried this exercise in class, Terry was the one to sit in the chair. After she got up, her classmate came into the room and sat down in Terry's empty chair. She described feeling fidgety and had a sense of insatiable curiosity. She also described feeling as if she wanted to write everything down. What she wrote described Terry exactly!

As you practice this exercise you will find that you gradually increase your psychic attunement, or sensitivity, to the residual magnetic energy left by another person.

Touching Hands

Sit opposite a friend or partner. Each of you rub your hands together and then place your palms against the other person's. What feelings are you picking up from your partner? Since all living things are continuously emanating various kinds of energy, touching another person's hands with the intention of feeling his or her energy is a way to help increase your ability to feel the energy in your own hands as well as the other person's. It's the same kind of energy that's used in Reiki healing techniques.

Intuitive Body Scanning

You will need a partner for this exercise. Begin by imagining yourself surrounded by a bubble of white or gold light for spirituality and protection. Ask your partner to lie down on a bed or floor mat. Place your hands on the other person's body, or hovering just above the surface of his or her body. Without trying to make a conscious decision, are you instinctively drawn to any particular area? (And no, we're not talking about anything remotely sexual here!) Do you feel heat ema- nating from any part of the other person's body? If so, what you're sensing could be a blockage of chi (life force or energy) or a problem area for the subject. Heat often indicates an illness or inflammation. When you feel something, ask your partner if he or she is holding tension or feeling pain in that particular area. With practice, you will find that your sensations are becoming more and more accurate.

Tell Me a Story

Ask your partner to focus on a past experience that has emotional sig- nificance for them. The point here is not to telepathically determine what the story is; instead, you want to notice the feelings you pick up while the other person is thinking about the incident. Afterward, share your impressions with your partner and get their feedback. Two things are likely to happen when you do that. They may be amazed by how accurately you reflect their feelings, or you may have been sensing emotions they had been hiding from themselves or trying to suppress. Many of us are cut off from our feelings, and clairsentients can feel what others may not be able to feel, such as anger, shame, guilt, and trauma. When you do this exercise, you will be surprised at how many emotions you pick up.

HOW CLAIRSENTIENT ARE YOU? TAKE THE QUIZ!

Answer yes or no to the following questions:

1. Are you sometimes overcome with a wave of emotion, sad- ness, or empathy for a person you have just met?
2. Do you get a gut feeling that something is wrong, that you want to run away from a person, or that something just doesn't feel right?
3. Do you feel overwhelmed or exhausted around large groups of people, such as in a shopping mall or at a crowded sport- ing event?
4. Do you feel happy when you're around children or animals?

5. Do you feel pain in some part of your body, such as your neck, back, or stomach, when you are with another person that gets better after that person leaves?
6. Do certain people at home or at work drain you of energy?
7. Are you sensitive to fluorescent lighting?
8. Are you more uncomfortable than most people to extremes of hot or cold?
9. When there is a natural disaster, do you sense the pain others may be feeling?
10. Can you feel energy from objects that belong to someone else (such as jewelry, a set of keys, or a cap), even if you don't know the owner?

Have you answered yes to five or more of these questions? If so, you are clairsentient. Being aware of your empathic tendencies will help you to protect yourself from inadvertently taking on the negative feelings of others. But clairsentience also increases your potential to act as a healer, and is therefore a gift to be cherished and developed.

So now that you know which of your Clairs are the strongest and how you can continue to develop them, the next section of the book is going to talk about the many tools we all have for opening our minds and honing our psychic abilities.

PART III

TOOLS FOR TUNING IN TO YOUR POWERS

By now you have a good idea which Clair is your strongest. We've given you some exercises to improve the skills you already have, as well as to develop those areas where you may not be as naturally psychic. Now we're going to provide the tools that will help you to open your mind and ramp up your overall psychic intelligence even more.

Depending on which of your Clairs is the strongest, you may find some of these tools easier to use than others. Or you may be more drawn to dream interpretation than automatic writing. You may feel more comfortable asking your angels for guidance than working with crystals or psychometry. That's fine. You get to choose the tools you want to work with. Nevertheless, we'll explain how to use all of them and more, because we want you to know that these tools are available to each and every one of us.

11

Angels, Spirit Guides, and Other Helpers in High Places

May I become at all times,
Both now and forever,
A protector for those without protection
A guide for those who have lost their way
A ship for those with oceans to cross
A bridge for those with rivers to cross
A sanctuary for those in danger
A lamp for those without light
A place of refuge for those who lack shelter
And a servant to all in need.

—from *Ethics for the New Millennium*,
by His Holiness the Dalai Lama

Angels are incorporeal celestial beings created by God or the Higher Power that have never lived on the human plane, and for that reason they are often called "thoughts of God" or "thoughts of love." They carry energies up and down, between dimensions, delivering celestial messages to us. And, by doing this, they respond to our spiritual and emotional needs, take care of us, and protect us.

In one of the best-documented modern instances of what appears to be true divine protection, fifteen members of the West Side Baptist Church choir in Beatrice, Nebraska, were spared serious injury or death in 1950 when the building exploded five minutes *after* the scheduled start of choir practice, because every single member, including the pastor, his wife and daughter, and the pianist, had been late for one reason or another—or for no apparent reason at all. It's not that any one of these people had a sense or premonition that something bad would happen if they arrived at the practice on time. They weren't late on purpose. They were simply, and uncharacteristically, delayed. To us, this is a clear case of angelic protection.

Many people have told us they don't believe they have a guardian angel because if they did, their angel would have protected them from the bad things that had occurred in their lives. The truth is that we all have guardian angels and spirit guides, but they can't protect us from every single negative experience because some of those experiences teach us lessons our soul is meant to learn. And, furthermore,

REASONS WE BLOCK OUR GUIDANCE

- As children, we may have picked up on disbelief from adults.
- We may be afraid of punishment.
- We don't think we can connect to our spirit guides.
- We don't know how to connect, or what questions to ask.
- We want a different answer.
- We are too busy and stressed, which slows our vibration.
- Drugs and alcohol can block the communication, creating a veil between ourselves and spirit.
- We are too focused on our "rational" or "logical" mind.
- Too much focus on the material world can block our intuitive powers.
- We see life as a "do-it-yourself project" and refuse to accept help.

ASK THE ARCHANGEL MICHAEL FOR HELP

Archangel Michael appears in the Hebrew, Christian, and Islamic religious traditions and is considered the commander of the angelic army; as such, he is extremely powerful. Like all angels, he is an extension of God or the Higher Power to which we all have access, and thus, through him, we all have access to God. You can call upon him as you would your guardian angels or spirit guides, through prayer or meditation, whenever you are faced with making a difficult decision or dealing with a difficult person or situation. He will give you physical strength and provide spiritual protection when you need it most.

if we choose to disbelieve in their existence, we may be cutting ourselves off from connecting with the guidance they are able to provide. If you close your eyes, you can't see where you're going; when you close your mind, you can't tune in to those signals that let you know where you *should* be going.

As we've said, we are all born with an awareness of angels, but then we become afraid of acknowledging them. Children are more aware of the angelic realm because they have not been conditioned to distrust what they feel, know, or see for themselves. Children are like pure antennae to receive information from the spirit world. As adults, we can reopen this awareness as we let go of our fears and learn how to be like children again—in a perpetual state of wonder and discovery.

If you are clairvoyant, you may notice angels as a moving light, patterns in your mind, or apparitions that appear in your dreams. Clairaudients tend to hear angelic voices providing them with guidance. As a clairsentient you may talk about feeling or sensing an angelic presence, and claircogs are likely to tell you that they just "know" their angels are watching over them. You may become aware of their presence in a time of need or great stress, just as you would that of a person who is standing near you in a room.

In fact, some angels do actually incarnate as human beings whose mission it is to help heal other people as well as the planet. Known as "earth angels," these people are all around you. They could be your grocer, your babysitter, your hairdresser, or the guy who washes your car. They tend to be kind and lovable, with an inner spiritual light and joy that cheers everyone around them. They come in all colors, sizes, and ethnicities and are often engaged in education, healing, counseling, or spiritual work.

What Are Spirit Guides and Are They Different from Angels?

Spirit guides differ from angels in that they have lived in human form. Often, a spirit guide will be a relative from an earlier generation, a teacher, or a loved one from a previous incarnation. We all have at least one spirit guide, and we may have several as we evolve and grow spiritually and psychically over the course of a lifetime. Both angels and spirit guides radiate beneficial energies and particular qualities of peace, love, and hope to us through their feelings. While angels can and do help unlimited numbers of people, simultaneously if necessary, your spirit guide is more personal to you because the guide has already had some earthly connection to you.

People sometimes ask how they can determine the identity of their spirit guides. You can do this by finding a quiet place, doing a meditation to focus your mind (for more on meditation, see Chapter Twelve), and asking your guide to connect with you. You can then pose simple questions about the guide's identity, such as a name (which can be difficult to understand if it is unfamiliar to you), whether you've met in a previous lifetime, or what relationship you have to one another. You can ask these questions aloud or simply with your thoughts, and the answers will come to you as thoughts, mind pictures, or through automatic writing (see Chapter Fourteen). Trust the answers you receive and write them down as soon as your communication is over so that you don't forget them. As you continue to meditate and practice connecting, you will become more aware of your spirit guide's positive and loving energy.

How Angels and Spirit Guides Communicate

One day several years ago, we had just finished a very powerful reading with a client and were taking a walk, as we do every day. We were still in something of a trance after the reading, when suddenly, a large bubble, almost like a soap bubble, appeared in front of us. It was an amazing experience and we followed it for many blocks, entranced, before the bubble disappeared. When we tuned in, we heard our guides tell us that it was a spirit named Aurelia, and that she wanted us to know we had her support.

In this case, Aurelia came to us unbidden, but we can also ask to connect with our spirit guides in order to seek advice, and they can help us by making subtle suggestions that steer us to the best solution or course of action. Sometimes they give us reassurance that we are already on the right path, or they encourage us to open up to a new opportunity. They cannot, however, interfere with our free will, which means that while they can assist us in seeing the best options, they can't make decisions for us.

Of course, you can't just pick up the phone and call up your angel or spirit guide, and the information they provide isn't going to be as obvious or direct as what you receive from a living human— although it very well might be better informed and useful because it comes from a higher level of knowing.

We previously wrote about a remarkable and uplifting symbolic message we received at a time when we needed it very much. Because of our ongoing health problems, we had been to see a well-known French psychic healer named Jean-Michel, whose work involves purifying energy fields in a variety of dimensions in order to elevate one's vibration and balance the soul. The day of our visit was damp and rainy and Terry was feeling particularly tired. We took turns sitting with him and describing our physical problems as he prayed and worked with us.

Afterward, his helper and translator told Linda that she had experienced a most unusual expansion during the session, that she was "moving out of the field of fear to become the light," and that her energy could now balance that of nine million people suffering on the planet.

Two days later, we were taking our daily walk in the beautiful hills of our neighborhood when Terry said a silent prayer to the angels and nature devas (spirits of nature) asking for a sign that we were on the right track with our work and our path to healing ourselves of lifelong illness. Within minutes a bright monarch butterfly circled us, followed by several more. Then, to our utter amazement, scores of butterflies swarmed out from behind the homes and trees on the hills, descending upon us by the hundreds, then thousands! They came out of nowhere, a magnificent colorful swirl of winged creatures that completely surrounded us, and their numbers increased as we walked another hour toward home. When we stopped other people and asked them about the butterflies, they said they did not see them! In fact, they were totally confused. The two of us were completely astonished, because no one else was able to see this vision. This was undeniably a powerful omen from our angelic guides letting us know that a great transformation had occurred for us. The butterfly phenomenon continued for two days, and just as quickly vanished. It was truly a sign of blessings to come, and it remains to this day one of the most magical experiences of our lives.

How to Connect with Your Angels and Guides

First of all, it should go without saying that you need to transcend your doubts and really believe that you *can* communicate with your angels and guides. Open yourself up to the expectation that when you ask for guidance, you *will* receive an answer. We wish that we could give you an easy formula for doing that, but different people have different reasons for fearing or doubting what they can't explain or prove. So, if you find yourself clinging to disbelief, we suggest that you reread Part One of this book, try to figure out what's holding you back, and follow our suggestions for letting go and opening up to a new way of thinking about your ability to communicate with the source of your higher intelligence.

When you're ready to connect, find a quiet, comfortable place where you feel relaxed and know that you won't be disturbed—that could be a beach, a park, a field of flowers, or even your own living room. Sit comfortably, close your eyes, and take a few deep breaths to quiet your mind. If you have trouble clearing your mind of random thoughts, try doing the Meditation to Surrender Control on pages 138–39. Now, with your eyes closed, focus on "seeing" your third eye, which is the sixth chakra, located in the center of your forehead, as you ask your angels and guides to surround you.

Now, silently ask for the guidance or information you seek. Your angels and guides hear your thoughts. Depending on which of your Clairs is the strongest, your guides may communicate with you through visual images, words, feelings, or thoughts. Their communications are often delivered in the form of symbols that we then translate through our human filters. You might, for example, have a feeling that you're being "nudged" in a certain direction, or that something is telling you to take a different path from the one you had originally planned. You can even ask your spirit guide to help you become more open to your intuition so you are more receptive to the information you receive.

What pops into your head may surprise you because your conscious thoughts had been going in a different direction. You may then start to doubt the validity of the message or to second-guess yourself. Part of opening yourself up to your psychic intelligence is letting go of any preconceived notions of what you want or expect to receive.

Angels Need Love and Laughter

Angels operate on the currency of love. They value and cherish it, and they evolve through receiving love, just as we do. So please remember to thank your angels for their service to you. They are not used to getting much appreciation! And you will also find that both angels and spirit guides have a wonderful sense of humor. They feel that we often take life too seriously and try to get us to lighten up!

For example, we have done many photo sessions over the years, one of which was in the Rose Garden in Los Angeles. It is a very magical setting and in several of the photos, an odd, geometric shape can be seen hovering directly between our heads. A shamanic healer told us that it is a dodecahedron (a geometric form with twelve flat faces), which is symbolic of choices. In other photos where our shoulders are touching, lights have appeared between us. In fact, many of our clients have sent us photos of themselves with family members in which tiny lights or "floating orbs" are present all around them. Those tiny lights are angels, and you, too, may find something like this in your own photographs, especially when there are children or very happy people in the picture.

Our friend Rhiannon, who is extremely clairaudient and has the gift of mediumship, is very much aware that her angels are all around her. She's told us that they have been known to move her jewelry around and even hide her brown-bag lunch! Sometimes our angels just like to play games with us to let us know they are around.

Many of our friends who are professional psychics have a great sense of humor. The two of us are constantly making each other laugh, which helps us to keep our vibration high, facilitate ideas, and elevate our psychic abilities. Humor will definitely attract more angelic energy to you, as will singing, dancing, and music.

Come to Your Senses: Messages Come in Many Guises

> The senses are like a reversible coat. They can go
> outside to the world, or inside to the soul.
> —Buddhist proverb

John Lennon's son, Julian, tells this poignant story about his father. "One of the things my father said to me was that should he pass away, if there was some way of letting me know he was going to be okay, or that we were all going to be okay, it was by in some way, shape or form presenting me with a white feather.... About eleven years ago I was on tour in Australia and I was approached by an aboriginal tribe who gave me a white feather and asked me to help them—which I was taken aback by."

Julian went on to make a TV documentary about the tribe and decided to set up the White Feather Foundation to aid aboriginals and other struggling people directly and by supporting other charities.

When he was asked whether the white feather was a message, he said, "That's difficult to say. But what it did do for me was to motivate me to do something positive and for me that is the most important thing."

We have long felt that John Lennon is a muse for us and our writing. We were just finishing this book on what would have been his seventieth birthday, and Linda asked him to show us that he was assisting us in our mission to spread peace in the world by leaving a feather for us as a sign. When we left our building that morning to take a walk, what did we see right on our doorstep but two identical gray hawk feathers! The hawk is the messenger of the gods, and for us this was an absolute acknowledgment that John really is with us.

Messages, as we've said, come in many forms, and you need to be alert to notice and acknowledge them. Here are some of the ways you may receive spiritual messages:

Olfaction: The Sense of Smell

Although we jokingly refer to olfactory sensations as "clair-smellience," the actual term for a psychic sense of smell is "clairalience," or the sensing of a spirit through smell.

Smell is one of our most direct and powerful senses—about ten thousand times stronger than our sense of taste. The olfactory system of our brain has the longest recall of all the senses.

You might get a sudden whiff of your mother's favorite Chanel No. 5 perfume, your dad's Old Spice aftershave, or Grandpa's cigar smoke when you're all alone in a place where those aromas do not occur. When that happens, it's a sign from your loved one that he or she is still very much with you. When there is no obvious source of a particular smell, such as the fragrance of lilacs, it is most likely coming from a spirit source. Our friend Michelle, for example, tells us that her late father loved the smell of orange blossoms, and she now often smells them in the unlikeliest of places. That's because her father is letting her know that he is still with her in spirit and aware of what's going on in her life.

Music or Songs on the Radio

You might be thinking of a loved one, turn on the radio, and hear the song your grandmother used to sing to you. We very often walk into a store and hear "Sentimental Journey," our parents' favorite song, coming over the speakers. Our father played it for Mom during her last days, and we always think of her when we hear it.

We've also received reports of people hearing bells or the sounds of music while they were in surgery or in some kind of accident. We believe these are signs that their loved ones in spirit are gathering around them in their time of need.

Mental Images, Symbols, or Pictures

Angels communicate with us in visual ways. Psychics and mediums who are predominantly clairvoyant will "see" many pictures or symbols in their mind's eye. It might be a rose, symbolic of love and purity; a cake to signify a birthday; or a ring, signifying an upcoming wedding. These symbols could relate to one's past life, something going on in the present, or a future event. Because we are visual artists, the two of us often visualize paintings we have yet to paint, or movies we want to make in the future.

If an odd image pops into your head for no apparent reason or when you've been thinking about something entirely different, see if you can figure out where it's coming from or what it might mean. Did the image have significance for a loved one who's passed over to the world of spirit? Does it have a significance for you that only your late mother or father would have known? Consider that it may be a symbolic message of support or guidance from someone in spirit watching over you. Again, there's no simple way to tell you how to determine if these images are coming from a higher source. Sometimes you just need to have faith that you "know what you know."

DÉJÀ VU ALL OVER AGAIN

"Déjà vu" is a French term meaning "already seen." It is the sensation of feeling certain that you've been someplace before or met someone before, but the circumstances of the previous experience are uncertain. You may even have a sense that you've had the very same conversation in some other place in time. This experience is usually accompanied by a compelling sense of familiarity, but also feels weird or eerie.

Although scientists have complex explanations related to brain function for why we have these sensations, we believe that they are often related to an experience we had in a previous life, to dreams we've had in the past, or even to an out-of-body experience. In other words, the reason the experience feels so familiar is that, even though you're not consciously aware of it, you really have already "been there, done that."

The two of us have déjà vu feelings quite often. They are kind of like remnants of dreams that suddenly surface, or distant memories that flash back to us when we are least expecting them. One such experience occurred when we were in Italy as art students and visited the stunningly beautiful Sistine Chapel in Rome. Gazing in awe at the paintings of Michelangelo, Terry had the strongest sensation of having lived in Rome before and painting frescoes in that life. Even her paintings took on the feeling and light of Renaissance frescoes for a while. In retrospect, we could only assume that she was recalling an experience she'd had in a previous incarnation.

Dreams

As we've already discussed, angels work with us in our dreams, bringing us words of comfort or the answer to a problem. Even when we are sleeping, our frontal cortex is active, which helps us tune in to higher levels of thinking and connecting. Ask for a sign or message before you go to sleep and the angels will bring you an answer. (For much more on the interpretation of dreams, see Chapter Thirteen.)

Electronic Events or Disturbances

Angels and spirits work with electricity to get our attention or remind us of their presence. Lights might go on and off for no reason, or an appliance might turn itself on or off. One woman told us her vacuum cleaner kept going on without her touching it. This may be because spirits pull from electricity to manifest on our dense vibrational plane. Some people have said that these spirits can even drain the energy from batteries to make themselves visible. A medium friend of ours once went to a haunted location, and everyone's camera equipment suddenly went dead at the same time. When Terry goes to the dentist's office, all the X-ray machines go on the fritz. The X-ray techs roll their eyes when they see her coming!

When young people pass away, they are more likely than older people to communicate through technology. They will often use computers, telephones, TVs, or even text messages to communicate with us from the other side. One friend of ours said that her daughter typed rows and rows of the phrase "I love you" across her computer after she crossed over, and she was delighted to know that her daughter was sending her love. After our friend Conner passed at the age of twenty-eight, he communicated with us by finding the eulogy we gave for him on our hard drive and making it appear on our computer screen!

The Princeton Engineering Anomalies Research lab has done studies that prove the subconscious mind can indeed affect electronic devices.

In fact, many people who have had a near-death experience (as well as some who haven't) find that, because of the magnetic energy they exude, they cannot wear watches without breaking them. A young man we know told us about a strange experience he'd had when a dozen streetlights went out one by one as he walked under them.

We both have always had a strange effect on electronic devices of every kind, and we've been told by the person who helps us with our computers that we have more peculiar problems than anyone else he's ever worked with. He's even made up an acronym for it: PEMI or psychic electromagnetic interference—the inexplicable and intermittent interference or disruption of electronics, particularly low-level functionality with respect to computers and other IT-specific devices. In other words, working with electronics can be a real bummer if you're psychic.

On one particularly strange and amusing occasion we were working with an Emmy award–winning technical director named Randy, who was putting together a promo reel to pitch us for a television pilot. Suddenly, as Randy was fast-forwarding the tape, the numbers on his tape deck inexplicably started going backward. He looked at us perplexed and said, "I have no idea what's going on! These numbers should be going up—not down!" As we sat there, he pressed various buttons and became even more mystified. "There are long stretches with no sound on both sides of the tape now. That can't be!" He turned the tape over again and punched play. No sound. Fast-forward again. Nothing. "This is *so* strange!" Randy muttered to himself. He knew he had not erased the tape.

"It's spirit interference," Linda said, laughing. "There are spirit energies here right now, playing games with us." Randy looked flustered but continued his tape dubbing. As we all listened to the playback of a series of world predictions we had made, the sound kept cutting out for no discernible reason. Randy looked at his wife, Debbie, baffled. "This is so *weird*," he muttered again. "I've never had this happen before."

"We always have this effect on equipment," Terry explained apologetically.

"It's called 'High Strangeness,'" Linda added. "High Strangeness" is a term that has been used in paranormal and UFO research for years to describe phenomena that defy the rules of conventional physics, things so peculiar that nobody can explain them.

About ten minutes later the tape went missing entirely. We looked everywhere, and eventually Randy found it under the sofa. How had it gotten there? Later, as we were leaving, the television suddenly went on by itself, blinking at us like a giant neon blue eye.

"What are you gals *doing*?" Randy exclaimed, wide-eyed. "The TV just went on, and I didn't even touch it! What's going on?"

"They're saying good-bye!" Linda replied as we went out the door laughing.

We all have angels and spirit guides around us all the time, and sometimes they just like to have fun with us to remind us of their presence. If these things happen to you, instead of getting annoyed, just tell yourself how lucky you are to have such a close psychic connection with those in the spirit world.

Bodily Movement

Often Linda's head will move slightly to the left or right during psychic sessions. She noticed early in her channeling work that spirit would move her head to the left if the answer was no and to the right if the answer was yes. You can train yourself to receive answers in this way by giving yourself an autosuggestion that encodes the command. This is very much the same as the pendulum work we described in Chapter One, except that your body will be acting as the pendulum. For example: Make the okay sign with your right thumb and forefinger pressed together while stating, "When the answer is yes, my fingers will hold together. When the answer is no, I will be able to pull them apart." Then ask a yes or no question, such as, "Is this medicine positive for me in this dosage now?" With your other hand, try to pull your fingers apart. If they pull apart easily, the answer is no.

Numbers

Angels and spirit guides sometimes give us messages through showing us sequences of numbers. They may show up on digital clocks, license plates, building addresses, dry-cleaning tickets, the flight number on your airline ticket, even the number of "friends" on your Facebook page!

Here are some examples of number sequences and their meanings. We've given them as three-digit sequences, but there can also be sequences of more than three of the same number, and they will have the same meanings.

When you see one of these sequences, try to notice what happened or what you were thinking about just before you saw the numbers. Your spirit helpers may be alerting you to pay attention to something specific that is going on in your life and reassess your options or the choices you've been making.

111—A sign of new beginnings, a doorway of opportunity opening up for you. The number 1 represents initiative and drive. You have the power to transform a situation if you focus on what you want. Stay in faith.

222—Represents the process of ideas becoming reality. It is symbolic of the process of creation, partnership, and cooperation. Seeing this sequence of numbers means that you are about to attain a long-held dream or wish. Manifestation is near. Keep affirming what you want.

333—Represents wholeness, unity, heaven, or the spiritual realms; symbolizes creativity, the feminine mystic essence, and clarity. Expect a successful solution to a problem you are facing.

444—Symbolic of initiation, also symbolizes the presence of angelic beings who want you to pay attention or wake up to a new way of doing things; 4 also represents mastery and willpower. A decision needs to be made.

555—Symbolic of the center, harmony, balance. It means order, perfection, a bridge between the physical and the spiritual. A major life change is imminent. It is a good time to seize new opportunities or promote your business. You will notice a freeing up of your energies.

666—Represents conflict or unrealized potential. Your thoughts are out of balance. You may be too wrapped up in ego and acquiring material trappings. Focus more on your spiritual side and being of service to others.

777—Represents the enlightened self, a fresh start, positive regeneration. A very spiritual number, 7 symbolizes mysticism, magic, and psychic energies. Your wishes are coming true, and yes, you are on the right path!

888—It is the number of infinity (∞). The sequence 888 indicates that a phase or cycle of your life is about to end, emotionally or professionally, and a new one is soon to begin. In Buddhism, 8 means "to open."

999—Means completion. You are at the end of a major phase of your life; 9 symbolizes the electrical energy of the cosmos. An auspicious number, 999 indicates a way through obstacles. There is a light at the end of the tunnel.

000—A reminder of your oneness with Source energy. Zero represents a cycle of rebirth, or the completion of a cycle of destiny. A situation has come to fruition for you, and you will soon taste the fruit of your labors.

In addition to sequences of the same number, you may also notice numbers appearing in ascending or descending sequences, such as 123, 234, 456 or 654, 432, 321. (The sequences can also be longer.) If you're considering a change in a particular area of your life, seeing ascending sequences of any denomination is generally a sign that following your thoughts will lead to a positive outcome. Seeing descending sequences is usually an indication from your spirit guides that following your thoughts will be taking a step backward or lead to a negative result.

Oracles and Omens

The word "oracle" is derived from the Latin word *"orare,"* which means "to speak." An oracle can be a tool for divination, or it can refer to the person interpreting the information through the use of a divining tool.

To receive guidance, knowledge, or illumination from a mysterious source beyond the personal self is called "oracular knowing." We know that oracles existed as far back as ancient Greece, and that the earliest of them were female priestesses known as "sibyls." In ancient times, people paid large fees to consult one of these oracles about important decisions. The oracle would retire to her chamber, enter a trance state, and then emerge to deliver her message. Sometimes, if the message was not to the seeker's liking, the oracle was killed. (Hence the saying, "Don't shoot the messenger.")

Thinking about it, we're probably lucky to be alive and kicking, given that we've delivered some pretty direct messages over the years! (Contrary to what some may believe, we do *not* drink virgin's blood, smoke anything, nor do we sit in a dark cave inhaling fumes to achieve a trance state. We live in L.A.—we get enough toxic fumes as it is!)

Oracular knowing creates a bridge of mystical connection between the personal soul and mysterious realities beyond the self. Socrates relied on oracles to guide him in his life decisions. Moses, Confucius, and Carl Jung all believed in the art of divination. Oracular divination in one form or another has been used in every culture throughout history and can still be found in many modern-day cultures, including African witch doctors, Haitian voodoo priests, and Asian shamans. In truth, however, any knowledge you receive from the world of spirit is oracular knowing, so, as you tune in to your own psychic intelligence, you, too, will become a kind of oracle.

An omen—as opposed to an oracle—is basically any sign or symbol that portends some kind of future occurrence. It can appear in any form, such as a dream or a sign from the world of nature—and if we don't have an oracle handy to interpret it for us, we need to be alert to recognize the sign when it occurs.

When the two of us take our daily walk, we pass by the reservoir that is near our home, and we sometimes see a beautiful white heron that appears only when we are about to experience a significant breakthrough in our business or personal life. The heron is always standing knee-deep in the rushing water and gleaming in the sun. Just recently we made a wonderful connection with someone by phone. After our chat, we took our usual walk and saw not one but *two* white herons—identical twins perhaps? In mythology white herons are said to be messengers of the gods that symbolize a change in luck (good or bad) and are also a sign of wealth. We believe our two white herons appeared as magical omens bringing us both a message of hope and good fortune! We've also seen eight ducks floating in the river in a perfect V formation. Eight is the symbol of infinity and opening, and ducks symbolize transition, grace, beauty, and sensitivity. Have you noticed any omens lately? We all receive these kinds of signs and symbols all the time; we just need to be open and aware so that we recognize them when they appear.

But, on the other hand, it's also important not to go overboard. Some people have a tendency to add significance to everything they see. If they see their boyfriend's first name on the side of a truck, for example, they automatically take this as an omen: "Oh, this must mean he's my soul mate!" Try to resist this tendency. Not every name or piece of music or animal appearance has symbolic significance. "Sometimes a cigar is just a cigar," as Freud may or may not actually have said. You may, for example, be thinking of marriage and see a photo of a wedding cake in a store window. This could mean that marriage is in your future or that someone around you is going to marry soon. But it could also mean that you just happened to be passing a bakery!

So how do you know the difference? You just need to be patient and wait until you have a result you can link to the omen. You may forget about it and then, within a few days or weeks, sometimes within hours, you'll get a confirmation of the omen. The important thing to look for is anything out of the ordinary. At first, you may chalk up an omen to mere coincidence, but the more you see them, the more you will begin to recognize them as affirmations from the spirit realm.

Once, when we were taking a walk we encountered a very nice lady who had her new dog, a border terrier, with her. We had started chatting about the dog when Terry noticed a large flock of crows swoop and land on a roof just in front of where we were standing. "Look at all those blackbirds!" Terry commented, and our new friend laughed and told us that she and her husband own two restaurants in the area with the name "Four and Twenty." There is an old nursery rhyme you may have heard: "Four and twenty blackbirds baked in a pie..." The crow is a powerful symbol of magic and healing and can indicate that something special is about to happen. We assumed this was a sign for the woman, but it turned out that a series of fortuitous events occurred for us later that week.

Animal Totems

Power animals, or animal totems, are animals with whom we identify spiritually and who have special lessons to teach us about life. Animal guides can reflect our own personal strengths and weaknesses and guide us through difficult times. They can also help to awaken our energies and shift our negative patterns. According to some traditions, the animal chooses the person who can benefit most from its particular energy and guidance.

Animal totems are associated with particular meanings. Here are some of those that are most common:

Bear: Introspection. Symbolic of the intuitive mind. The bear helps you to look inward to discover your true goal. Hibernate with your ideas or projects until the time is right. The bear is also a symbol of power. You may need to defend your beliefs.

Buffalo: Abundance, grace, courage, creativity, honoring your path, and strength of character. The white buffalo is considered the most sacred of animals in many Indian traditions. It is a sign that prayers are being heard and signals a time of abundance.

Butterfly: Symbolic of joy and transformation. Brings clarity or organization. The butterfly can show you the next step in your personal life.

Cat: A link to the tiger or lion family. The cat symbolizes wholeness, and teaches that the spiritual and physical realms are one, not separate worlds.

Crow: The guardian of magic and healing. When there are crows around, you can be certain that something special is about to happen.

Deer: Associated with unconditional love, gentleness, innocence, and compassionate action. It represents our connection with our inner child.

Dog: A link to the wolf, the dog symbolizes protection and loyalty, as well as the ability to accept life and its challenges.

Dolphin: Symbol of breath, sound, kindness, play, intelligence, communication, and awareness.

Eagle: Represents a state of grace—seeing beyond the mundane world to your greater purpose—achieved through hard work, understanding, and trials. The eagle is the symbol of success, wealth, freedom, and courage.

Fox: Teaches us detachment, to be alert, and to observe with our intuitive sense so that we know when to act. We need to be clever, but patient and very discreet.

Hawk: Messenger of the gods. Trains you to be the observer. The hawk invites you to seek the truth and be more aware. A hawk could foretell the birth of a child, or a problem coming into your life.

Lion: Symbolic of courage and heart-centered leadership, the lion presents a lesson about wisdom in dealing with groups and teaches us to trust our creativity, intuition, and imagination.

Raccoon: The raccoon's "mask" symbolizes the fact that none of us are ever quite what we seem—even to ourselves. Raccoon wisdom can help us to understand the nature of disguise and to change our own identity when that is appropriate.

Skunk: A sign of self-respect, courage, willpower, and self-confidence. Skunk wisdom represents learning how to "walk your talk" and being assertive. It teaches us to repel those who try to steal our energy or disrespect us. Skunk medicine can also be a sign of sexual healing.

Snake: Signifies transmutation. It is the power of creativity, sexuality, and alchemy. The snake is the energy of cosmic consciousness and teaches you that you are a universal soul. It tells you to let go of things that are no longer useful.

Squirrel: Represents being prepared and the ability to plan ahead. Also symbolizes letting go of negative, limiting beliefs.

Tiger: The tiger represents passion and sensuality. It also symbolizes being focused on the present moment. The tiger brings forth a quiet, solitary power.

Turtle: The turtle teaches us to be careful in new situations and to take things slowly so that we can develop our thoughts and ideas and figure out how to protect ourselves or move ahead.

Whale: Represents our deeper awareness and emotions. This totem represents personal power and teaches us to listen to our inner voice and to trust our wisdom.

Wolf: Teacher; the pathfinder. The wolf is about exploring hidden aspects of your consciousness. It teaches you to develop strength, balance, and confidence in your decisions so that you don't lose your identity.

WHICH ANIMAL ARE YOU DRAWN TO?

Is there an animal or bird you feel most drawn to? Have you noticed a recurring animal in your dreams? Does a particular animal or bird seem to have your own personality characteristics? Sometimes very intuitive people are drawn to cats, for example, because they have an other-worldly quality and seem to know a secret that we don't.

The following meditation may help you to access your own animal totems:

- Take a moment to center yourself with three deep breaths in and out.
- Visualize a bright light shining ahead, and see yourself walking toward it.
- Imagine that you are approaching the doorway to an unseen realm.
- Open the door, and see a beautiful forest, with flowers and lush foliage everywhere. As you take in the beauty of the forest, imagine a winding path and begin to walk down this path.
- Pause for a few moments and quietly invite your animal guide to appear. What animal do you see? Is there more than one? What does this animal say to you? Is there a message? Ask him what chakra he is protecting, or any other question you might have.
- Thank your power animal and promise that you will return. Now say good-bye and retrace your steps up the path and back through the door.

Write in your journal whatever you can recall of your animal visit, and any messages or words you exchanged or received. As you compare your experience with the list of animals and their meanings on pages 131–33, you will become more adept at interpreting the messages they are delivering to you.

Believe and They Will Come

Whatever form it takes, divine guidance is normal. Relax and believe that you, too, can reclaim the gift of connection. There are angels in charge of every aspect of our lives: our careers, our homes; angels of love who arrange relationships; healing angels—even angels in charge of real estate! Call on a specific angel for whatever you need. They want to help us—it's in their job description!

12

Learn to Meditate

Most people do not take the time to just be quiet and listen. We took a walk near the beach the other day and saw a guy riding a bike while talking on a cell phone. A few minutes later a woman almost ran us over with her van while—you guessed it—talking on her cell phone! These days, even little children have cell phones.

Today, it seems that we're connected all the time through one electronic means or another. Sadly, however, this means that we've become a lot less connected to nature, to our environment, to one another on more than a superficial level; and, most important of all, we are less connected to our own intuition. Because we're so constantly distracted (by call waiting when we're in the middle of a conversation or by a BlackBerry going off when we should be paying attention to our dinner companion), we've become less able to focus on the things that really matter, and that could make the biggest difference in our lives—the signs and signals our higher intelligence is trying to deliver.

Twintuition Tip:
Just because you're in a room with someone (or even at the same table) doesn't mean you're actually present.

When we were kids, we had none of these technological gadgets and somehow we managed to survive. Kids growing up now are literally addicted to technology, which we firmly believe is going to negatively impact their ability to make real connections with real people in the here and now. To us, all that texting, e-mailing, and instant messaging are simply ways to avoid being truly intimate and tuning in to the energies and feelings of other people. That lack of connection is what contributes to the breakdown of all our relationships: social, marital, business, and communication with family. As a modern culture, we have lost the art of human connection, which is the basis for psychic intelligence. One thing most psychics agree on is that the best way to block out distractions, focus your mind, and increase your psychic intelligence is through meditation.

When you meditate, you can ask to receive answers or guidance from your intuitive mind, your Source, God, higher awareness, angels, inner wisdom—or whatever you prefer to call it. The answers, as discussed in the previous chapter, may come in the forms of symbols, words, pictures, feelings, sounds, music, even smells. Learning to recognize and interpret those answers will allow you to develop your receptivity to psychic information.

Many people tell us that they have tried meditating and find they can't sit still or focus long enough. But that's exactly the point, and these are the people who need to meditate the most! In our society, we're so scattered and intent on multitasking all the time that we feel guilty about taking even a few minutes to be in a place of stillness. It seems selfish. But the truth is, if we do not take time to recharge or revitalize at the deepest level of our mind, we are not much good to anyone. Think of your mind as a battery that will run forever if you take care of it and recharge it regularly. You recharge your cell phone, don't you? Aren't your mind and body worth whatever time and effort it takes to keep your life running smoothly?

Create Your Own Meditation Space

You may want to set up a small altar in a quiet room where you won't be disturbed. This will be your peaceful refuge, a safe retreat from the outside world. Our altar is a vintage dresser we painted pale yellow. We have our Buddhist scroll (the Gohonzon) in a sacred box or cabinet (the butsudan). As symbolic offerings, we have two white candles, a dish of incense, cut greens in a small vase, a plate of fruit, and a cup of fresh water. To us as Buddhists, these items symbolize the basic elements we need to sustain us (food and water) and to engage our senses (candles and incense). And the evergreen is a reminder of the eternity of life. But if you are not practicing Buddhism, your altar can hold whatever articles are inspirational, personal, and meaningful to you (for example, a photograph of a spiritual teacher or family members, healing crystals and stones, or any object that has magical meaning for you).

We have friends whose altars are as big and shiny as a new Cadillac, but this is not necessary. Your pure heart and sincere faith are what count. When we first started to help beginners learn the practice, we used to tack cardboard shirt boxes to the wall as makeshift butsudans to hold their Gohonzons, and we used storage crates covered with a simple white cloth or silk scarf for our altars. The simplest gesture is enough.

A MEDITATION TO SURRENDER CONTROL

1. Sit in a quiet place and focus your attention on a problem or decision for which you need assistance.
2. Breathe in slowly to the count of seven, and exhale slowly to the count of seven.
3. Ask your higher self or spirit guide for help with a particular problem or area of concern.

4. Say: "I trust that whatever answers come into my mind are what I need to hear."

5. Visualize a ball of orange light above your head. Breathe in the light, bringing it down into your heart and then into your lower abdomen, the second chakra (your creative chakra), so that the energy is not so "stuck" in your head.

6. Surrender worry, or your attachment to hearing a particular answer.

7. Listen for a few minutes for any insights that may come into your mind from the spirit realm. Try not to judge them or latch on to any particular thought. Don't look for any "bolts from the blue." Sometimes what comes into your mind will seem like your ordinary thoughts. For example: "I should try to visit Mom this weekend." Or, "I wish the kids would clean up their rooms. I'm terrible with discipline." Or, "I wonder if my boyfriend is having an affair. He's been acting so weird lately." Let them float by like "leaves in a stream." You can also project the thoughts onto a mental movie screen and see them fading away. Other times, spirit will give you ideas or creative solutions to problems that your conscious mind may not have thought of. These thoughts tend to be very positive, simple, and comforting. For example, we used to be very anxious, with many worries. But our angelic thoughts, unlike our conscious thoughts, were always quite optimistic. Meditation would lift us out of our emotional quagmire with thoughts that were uplifting and encouraging, even when we were in deep distress or physical pain.

8. Imagine that your problem is resolving as you relax and bring more light into your heart and body.

9. After a few minutes, thank your spirit guide or Higher Power for the assistance you've been given.

Meditation, Not Medication

Wordsworth called meditation "a happy stillness of mind." For us it was a life raft. We were struggling with a boatload of challenging health issues that included cancer, fibromyalgia, chronic fatigue syndrome, and constant migraine headaches. We now believe that some of these illnesses were due to our taking on the pain of others in an effort to heal them. But, whatever the cause, even on our best days we felt like we had been run over by a Mack truck. What made matters worse was that medication failed us completely. An army of doctors gave up on us. One doctor called us "walking miracles" because, he said, he had never before met anyone who had survived so many life-threatening illnesses. Coupled with the financial problems we had at the time, we felt as though we had made the *Mis*fortune 500 list! To deal with the pain, we have practiced meditation in one form or another for almost thirty years now, and we know for a fact that it helps. For us it has literally been life-changing.

We have often described the function of meditation by comparing it to a workout at the gym. Meditation develops your "metaphysical muscles." When we first moved to New York City right after college, we were flat broke but rich in creative ideas. Our minds and emotions were all over the map. We were doing a hundred things at once: performing, designing costumes, painting, moving, and Terry was newly married at the time. When a nutritionist suggested that we try meditation, it felt strange and weird. We tried it, but it didn't come easily. Over the years, however, it has become our comforting friend and an absolute necessity for keeping us balanced and grounded in the face of myriad challenges. Now we can't believe anyone gets through life without it!

We always tell our students to try to find ten to twenty minutes in the morning at a set time to meditate. Try to be consistent, but don't beat yourself up if you aren't. You can always get back on track tomorrow. Today many people seem to feel that they have to be in control of every aspect of their life every minute of every day, which is, of course, impossible. Meditation is a way to give up some of that false sense of control, so the last thing you need is to use this as one more thing you have to do perfectly! Be patient with yourself. You will probably go through resistance in the form of boredom, anxiety, anger, and frustration as your ego fights for control. You may even begin making mental lists of errands you need to do, or friends you'd like to call. Or you may start planning dinner, which gets you thinking about that little Chinese restaurant where you had the great chow mein last week. When your attention wanders, bring your thoughts back to your breath. Distractions are normal, so just notice how much your mind darts around in its effort to avoid being present to what is. Keep challenging yourself to be in the stillness, and bring your mind back to your center each time it wanders. Mini "mindfulness meditation breaks" during the day can help you to keep your cool. Research has shown that even five minutes of meditation per day (outdoors or indoors) can reduce your stress levels.

Twintuition Tip:
Stressing about meditation just
adds to your stress.

A MEDITATION TO RELAX AND HEAL
THE BODY, MIND, AND SOUL

When you do this (or any meditation), make sure you are wearing comfortable clothing and that you have a quiet place where you won't be disturbed to sit or lie down.

1. Start to imagine that your body is slowly filling with white or gold light, starting from your feet and slowly moving up through your body.
2. As the light is moving up your body, begin to feel all of your muscles relaxing.

(Continued)

3. Feel the light moving upward until your entire body is filled with light. Now begin to direct the light toward any area of the body that is giving you pain or discomfort. Send extra light to this particular area.
4. Now shine a loving, healing light on the painful areas. Notice how you feel.
5. Imagine the tension and pain melting out of your body. Feel your muscles start to relax.
6. Now imagine radiating this healing light out to the world.
7. Begin to feel that this healing light is returning you to a state of health and balance.
8. Say aloud: "I am now restored to a state of perfect health and vitality. I am relaxed and balanced."

Use Guided Imagery to Help You Focus

There are many forms of meditation, many ways to reach that quiet place within yourself. One way we have found to be most successful for our students is to use what is called visualization or guided imagery.

Find a quiet place to sit comfortably (perhaps cross-legged on a pillow in front of your altar, or in a comfortable chair), and visualize yourself in a beautiful green field or a grove of trees, surrounded by flowers and a flowing brook. Try to make your environment as richly visual as possible using all of your senses. What do you hear, see, and smell? What does the ground feel like? After a minute, visualize yourself walking over to a package that is wrapped up like a gift. Hold a question in your mind to which you are seeking an answer. Allow your excitement to build as you approach the gift box. See yourself peeling off the wrapping and ribbons as you open the box. Trust that it holds the answer to your question. An answer will pop into your head that may be either clear or symbolic of something that doesn't quite make sense. Thank your angels for the gift and return to your peaceful place of solitude.

Over the next few days, you will notice things that relate to or clarify the message you received. Our friend Artie calls this "fab synchro timing." It may be a conversation in which someone gives you a suggestion or a sign of some kind. It may come in as a song playing on the radio, or something said on TV that will give you more clarity. You will find that your intuitive voice comes in more frequently to guide you on your path as you build your intuitive skills.

Try to Be More Mindful

The Buddha was once asked, "What do you and your disciples practice?" He answered, "We sit, we walk, and we eat." The questioner was confused. "Doesn't everyone sit, walk, and eat?" he asked. "Yes," replied the Buddha, "but when we sit, we know we are sitting. When we walk, we know we are walking. When we eat, we know we are eating."

The Lama Surya Das, a highly trained, Western-born priest in the Buddhist tradition, suggests that there are many ways in which we can become more mindful as we go about our day. We try to follow his wise suggestions, and we would urge you to do the same.

1. When you wake up in the morning, remind yourself what it means to be truly aware.
2. As you brush your teeth, look in the mirror and give yourself a smile to start your day.
3. While you're standing in the shower, take a few moments to relax and feel the water washing your mind clean so that you can live completely in the moment.
4. Mindful eating is a practice central to Buddhism. As you eat your breakfast, focus on the taste, texture, and aroma of the food. Imagine the food you are eating nourishing your body.

5. As you drive to work, notice whether the sun is shining. Pay attention to your surroundings. Too often we start to think about all the things on our to-do list and fail to notice what we're doing at the moment.

6. Take time during your day to stop what you're doing and look out the window. Use this time to regain your balance and center yourself.

7. When you return home, take a moment before going inside to appreciate the full circle you have made. Rejoice in your homecoming.

It is amazing how often we allow our inner voice to be drowned out by all the external noise in our lives. If we can take those moments to quiet our thoughts and be present with ourselves, we'll be much more likely to hear what our psychic intelligence is trying to tell us instead of ignoring, discounting, or contradicting it. Practicing meditation on a regular basis is one of the surest ways we know to do that.

13

Be a Dream Weaver

Dreams are the secret, symbolic language of our subconscious mind. Since earliest recorded history, people have theorized about why we dream. Many believe the function of dreams is to express the unconscious mind and process the emotions and thoughts we don't give ourselves permission to express in our waking state. Just as we can train ourselves to become more open to receiving spirit messages during our waking hours, we can train ourselves to have greater access to higher "knowing" through our dreams.

There are many well-known stories of scientists' having made intuitive leaps that allowed them to solve previously insoluble problems as a result of something they dreamed. Friedrich August Kekulé, a prominent nineteenth-century chemist, claimed to have discovered the chemical structure of benzene as the result of a dream. According to Kekulé, he had done numerous failed experiments before having a dream in which a snake took its own tail in its mouth, causing him to suddenly understand the ring-like structure of the benzene molecule.

One morning Stephenie Meyer, a stay-at-home mother of three young sons, woke up from a dream about people she couldn't get out of her head. When she sat down at her computer to write, Meyer said the story came to her easily. While spending her days potty training and taking her boys to swim lessons, she continued to write late into the night when the house was quiet. Three months later, she finished her young-adult romance novel, *Twilight*, which went on to become a huge international best seller and a blockbuster motion picture—and it all started with a dream!

And Paul McCartney has said that he composed the entire melody for "Yesterday" in a dream.

Dreams can also be "precognitive," telling us about something that will happen in the future. Before she died, our mother had been very ill with Alzheimer's disease for ten years. Just before she died, we had spent a deeply emotional day with her and other family members, and fell asleep after midnight, exhausted. Terry then was suddenly startled awake with the vision of Mom passing before her like an angel. She woke up Linda and said, "Mom's gone." Shortly after that we got the call from our father, confirming that Terry's dream vision had occurred just moments before Mom passed.

Call Upon Your Dream Masters

Dream masters are angels who are in charge of your dreams. You can call on them at any time and ask them for help in providing you with solutions or creative ideas. Some psychics suggest placing a smooth quartz crystal on your forehead, or "third eye," before sleeping and engaging in a short meditation asking to receive an answer to an important question or decision you have to make. Black obsidian and amethyst can also help to unblock your subconscious mind. Or you might try using essential oils, which are known to have healing properties. Try putting a few drops of lavender, Roman chamomile, valerian, cedarwood, orange essence, or frankincense in your bathwater, or blend a few drops into a lotion and rub it on the bottoms of your feet before bed to help you sleep and dream. We have found that these tools help our clients access dream knowledge, but you should experiment to find what works best for you.

If there is a question you would like to have answered or a

problem you need to solve, asking for the answer or the solution as you drift off to sleep may bring about a dream that provides the information you are seeking either during the dream itself or immediately upon awakening.

You can also ask to receive a dream about your future. It does help to be specific about the topic—and be open to receiving the information from your angels. The results may surprise you! For example, if you are trying to choose between two college majors, ask for a dream that will clearly show you the best course of action. Or if you cannot decide between two cities to live in, ask that the best location be revealed in your dream. Once again, you are exercising your metaphysical muscles here, and the more you pay attention to your intuitive guidance, the clearer the information you are bound to receive.

In addition to bringing us answers, dreams are among the most powerful tools we have for connecting with our loved ones in spirit. Before you go to sleep, ask your dream master or dream angels to assist you in making a connection with the person from whom you would like to have a "dream visit." When you wake up, write down whom you saw, noticing colors, shapes, dark or light images, and visual sensations. Was the image clear or fuzzy? In color or black and white? Two- or three-dimensional? What was the person wearing? Were there clear details like eyeglasses, hair done up in a bun? What kinds of feelings did you have? Was the person speaking to you, or giving some kind of a message? All these details are like pieces of a puzzle that, when put together, will describe the person or spirit who has tried to communicate with you. Too often we dismiss these dreams out of hand, but why would you want to do that? It would be like slamming the door in the face of a friend or family member who has come to say hello!

Of course, you may also have dreams about someone who has died that are not actually dream visits. In that case, there may be some aspect of the person you've dreamed about that you need to look at, or an unresolved issue with him or her that is coming up for a reason. It is worth taking the time to meditate on what the message is when you have the time.

A MEDITATION TO ENCOURAGE DREAMS

Before you fall asleep, try this dream meditation. It may help to record these words in your own voice and play the tape before you go to bed:

"My dreams influence me in a healing way. They restore and renew me. New patterns are being revealed to me in my dreams. All my negative emotions or destructive beliefs are revealed as undesirable through my dreams. My dreams invigorate me and help me to express my optimum potential. I am more aware than I ever imagined being. The information that I need flows easily in my dreams. Good things flow to me from many directions. My dreams help me to expand my consciousness. When I awaken, I will have the solution to my problem. Thank you, I am at peace."

Keep a Dream Journal

As you begin to cultivate your dream knowledge and become more aware of your dreams, it's important that you keep a dream journal. Have a notebook next to your bed so that you can record your dreams in as much detail as possible as soon as you wake up—and before they fade from memory. The more you do this, the better you'll be able to remember and the more adept you'll become at tapping into your own psychic intelligence by learning to interpret the signs or symbols you receive in your dreams.

Your journal will provide you with a record you can look back on to review your progress, see patterns of repetitive dreams, and verify your predictions. Journaling also helps you get more in touch with the feelings, thoughts, and emotions connected with your dreams. It enhances awareness and mindfulness, and actually helps you to overcome creative blocks and fears. With practice, it will become second nature.

WHY CAN'T YOU REMEMBER?

If you find that you have difficulty remembering your dreams, there may be some blocks you can dissolve. Ask yourself the following questions:

- Am I afraid I'll have nightmares?
- Am I afraid that if I dream it will disrupt my restful sleep?
- Am I afraid that frightening images like spiders or fire might appear in my dreams?
- Am I afraid of having a negative vision about my future or someone else's that may be scary for me?
- Am I afraid that if I see something scary it will really happen?

If you answered yes to any of these questions, release any fears that may be preventing you from making the most of your dreams. You can do this by journaling about what it is you may fear, by meditating to release your fears, or by repeating one or more of the following affirmations:

- I easily recall my dreams.
- I call upon my dream angels to protect me from nightmares.
- I ask for beautiful and healing dreams tonight.
- Angels come to me in my dreams and guide me.
- I am safe as I dream.
- I dissolve all fear.
- I ask to see and know only positive information.
- I am always protected from negative dreams.
- My dreams give me inspiration.
- My dreams are always pleasant and uplifting.

Interpreting Your Dreams

Our dreams provide us with symbols and images that, if interpreted correctly, will help us to change our life path. Some of the most commonly reported dreams involve flying or falling, sexual experiences and embarrassing moments, being chased, running without getting anywhere, and people being alive when we know they are actually dead. All these "dream themes" have symbolic significance, which we'll be discussing in detail later in this chapter. Once you become aware of their symbolic meanings, your dreams will provide you with important clues about a direction you should (or shouldn't) be taking in your life and help you to get in touch with your subconscious and intuitive thoughts. Once those subconscious thoughts and feelings are made conscious, you will be able to examine them, determine whether or not they are serving you well, and whether you need to change them or take heed of what they're trying to tell you. If, for example, you dream that you are falling, it may be a sign that you feel as if some aspect of your life is out of control. By becoming aware of that, you can take the steps necessary to regain the control you have lost. Running without getting anywhere can be taken as a warning that you need to change directions in order to move ahead in your career or a personal relationship.

One of the reasons it's so important to keep a dream journal is so that you can look back on your dreams, think about the messages you've received, and determine how to respond to them.

DREAM INTERPRETATION IN THE ANCIENT WORLD

In some ancient cultures, such as those of Greece, Rome, Mesopotamia, and Egypt, dream interpretation was valued as a sacred healing technique. Temples with sacred sleeping chambers were attended by high priests and priestesses who were trained in a process called "incubation." Patients were given purifying baths, massaged with essential oils, and then taken to the sleeping chamber. The following morning, the patient would recount his dream and the healer would interpret it in detail.

Have a Dream Party

It can be both fun and enlightening to get together with a small group of like-minded people and practice interpreting one another's dreams.

Have each person write down on a piece of paper one or two vivid or recurring dreams he or she has recently experienced. Put all your dream papers in a hat and pass the hat around. Each person will give their interpretation of the dream they have picked from the hat and try to guess who the "dreamer" is. Keep an open mind; you will be amazed by how accurate these interpretations often are—and how good you are at interpreting someone else's dream.

That said, however, dreams are very personal, and the best interpreter of your own dreams is you. Your dreams can enrich your psychic intelligence and serve as a kind of doorway to your past and future. The more you practice, the better you will get at discerning meaning from the symbols you dream about.

Do You Dream of Animals?

In Chapter Eleven we discussed the significance of specific animal totems. Beyond the kind of animal, however, what the animal is doing and how you relate to it in your dream will also have something important to tell you about your most basic instincts, strongest emotions, and deepest desires. If you have a dream involving an animal, try to remember:

- Whether the animal was wild or tame. A wild animal may indicate that you are in emotional turmoil or that you are feeling threatened in your daily life. It could also indicate that you should adopt a new perspective on a situation. A tame animal could mean that you are in a peaceful place in your life.
- If the animal was abandoned, abused, and neglected or healthy and well cared for. Abandonment or abuse could be an

indication of how you, yourself, are feeling, or it may reflect your fear that you will not be able to care for someone else. A healthy animal could reflect your own restored health.

- Whether you were interacting with the animal or only observing it. Interaction may indicate a willingness on your part to engage with someone in your life. Observing the animal from a distance would possibly mean detachment from a person or problem.
- Whether the animal was moving or standing still. To dream of an animal running toward you or behaving in a menacing way indicates that you feel violated or taken advantage of in some way. The dream may be symbolic of someone around you who is insensitive or cruel, or someone who may betray you. It may be a relative, friend, or significant other who has control over you despite your attempts to free yourself from the unhealthy relationship. An animal moving away from you indicates that the problem is not an immediate threat and is weakening in power. An animal standing still is an indication that there is no reason for you to make a hasty decision or take immediate action; you have time to think about whatever issue is bothering you before deciding what to do. If you are the one running away from the animal, you may be unwilling to confront some painful aspect of your subconscious mind. Meditate on whether or not there is some destructive emotion you are not willing to acknowledge.

When you consult the dream journal you've been keeping, consider how the details of your animal dream might relate to a particular situation, relationship, or problem in your life. How might your dream message affect the way you choose to deal with it? Use what you've learned in your dream to enhance your psychic intelligence, and trust that the wisdom you've received will help you to make the best decision for yourself.

Some Common Dream Symbols and What They Mean

The following are some of the more common dream symbols and their most generally accepted interpretations. As you begin to interpret your own dreams, you may find that a particular symbol has a slightly different meaning for you, or that you dream of something, someone, or some situation that is not included here. If so, as you continue to pay attention to your dreams, you will find that you become more and more adept at interpreting the meanings they have for *you*.

Apocalyptic events like a tsunami or earthquake may indicate that you feel out of control and/or emotionally overwhelmed in your personal life and may be resisting positive change.

Having an argument may mean that parts of your psyche are in conflict. Reexamine where you might be holding contradictory thoughts or feelings.

A baby or having a baby can be a sign of rebirth.

Being chased indicates that someone is making you feel threatened or may signify an emotional problem you don't want to face.

Being killed suggests that a significant relationship has ended and you are trying to separate yourself from emotion, but it can also mean that you are entering a new phase or beginning in your life.

Being lost or trying to find your way in a dream may mean that you are feeling trapped or disempowered in real life, unable to make the right choices.

Birds can signify good fortune or positive news. If flying, a bird can mean that you will be reaching new heights or achieving greater success in some aspect of your life.

Cats symbolize the feminine essence and are representative of your intuitive self.

Colors

Blue symbolizes liberation.

Lavender symbolizes refinement and grace.

Pink represents innocence, kindness, and unconditional love.

Black can be a dark omen symbolizing danger, loss, or death.

Brown represents an abundance of money.

Bright red represents the need to control your temper.

Deep red foretells good news.

Green represents heart energy, healing.

Yellow stands for personal empowerment and self-worth.

Death dreams are not always a bad omen. Like dreams of being killed, they can signify the death of an old pattern, belief system, or way of being. To dream of a coffin may be a precognition of the death of a friend or family member.

Drowning signifies fear of the unknown, or a sense of being unable to deal with a challenge you are facing. Your emotions are overwhelming you. Water has to do with relationships, and big waves can indicate anger or feelings of jealousy.

Falling symbolizes fear of failure, uncertainty, overwhelming emotions, or loss of control. You may need to address your fears or a situation that is out of control in your life right now.

Fire is a symbol of transformation. Flames can mean a burning of barriers that stand in your way. You'll soon take a turn for the better, change your circumstances, or heal from an illness.

Floating can mean you are in harmony with your emotions. It can also indicate feeling in alignment with your intuition.

Flying represents your ambition. If you are struggling to reach a higher altitude, you may be aiming too high. Flying can also mean moving beyond one's actual physical limitations.

Horses can symbolize freedom, or an expanded sense of self.

Illness can mean that you are emotionally hurt or fear being hurt. It may also warn of an upcoming risk to you or a loved one.

Jealousy can indicate insecurity, or feeling left out. Work on your self-acceptance.

Keys are symbolic of a spiritual opening. They can also foretell finding an answer to a problem.

Marriage can mean integration of the masculine and feminine aspects of yourself.

Mirrors symbolize truth or self-realization, but they can also be symbolic of vanity or superficiality. Dreaming of a mirror may be a sign that you are reflecting on your image and how you want people to see you.

Nightmares are our way of healing unresolved issues. They are shining a light on an aspect of our health or relationships that may need deeper work.

Nudity signifies an underlying fear of exposure or vulnerability. How are your life circumstances causing you to feel anxiety? Maybe you are about to start a new job and are feeling unprepared.

Paralysis could signify that you feel unable to act in a given situation, perhaps having to do with a love relationship. You may feel blocked or inhibited. What are you afraid to do?

Rain means a blessing is coming. Also, rain can symbolize cleansing or purifying. Water entering your home means that you'll be receiving a great deal of money in a month or two.

Rings symbolize friendship, marriage, or the completion of a cycle.

Running can mean fear of a situation in which you are not sure of yourself or an acceleration of events in your life.

Snakes often indicate that you will soon undergo a major internal change or come to a realization of your own power. They symbolize self-renewal and transformation.

A swimming pool can mean emotion, intuition, or the need to examine deeper realms of self.

Everybody Dreams Differently

It's true. We all dream, whether or not we remember our dreams—which means that we all have access to the wisdom that comes to us when we are sleeping. And the way we dream and what we remember may provide important information about our psychic intelligence.

Clairvoyants tend to have much more visual dreams, and to dream in color. Some people do not dream in color at all and may not see their dream unfolding in movies or pictures. Clairaudients are more apt to hear music or voices. The two of us sometimes hear entire sentences and conversations in our dreams, and other people have told us that they do as well. Clairsentients tend to recall the emotions and feelings attached to their dreams, and claircognizants, like clairvoyants, are those most likely to have dreams of something that is to happen in the future. So, *how* you dream may be a clue as to which Clair is your strongest.

14

Practice Automatic Writing

Automatic writing is a way to access all the ideas, knowledge, and wisdom of the Universe in order to receive guidance, advice, solutions to problems, and even knowledge of the future. It is considered the most reliable way to connect with what are sometimes referred to as the Akashic Records, or Akasha, a compendium of all knowledge that exists on a nonphysical plane, much like a cosmic library or universal filing system.

THE POWER OF *KŪ*

In Buddhism, the Akasha is known as *kū*, which translates to mean "void" but also means "sky" or "heaven." *Kū* represents those ethereal things beyond our mundane experience, particularly those things made of pure energy such as spirit, thought, and creative energy. It represents our ability to think and to communicate, as well as our creativity. It is associated with power, spontaneity, and inventiveness.

In martial arts where the fighting discipline is blended with magic, the warrior invokes the power of *kū*, or "nothingness," in order to connect to the quintessential creative energy of the Universe. A warrior attuned to the state of *kū* can sense his surroundings and act intuitively, without using his physical senses.

The process of automatic writing involves consciously shifting your mind in order to achieve an expanded state of consciousness that is called a "conscious trance." This is a kind of heightened consciousness in which you are able to bypass critical judgment and access a higher level of knowing. When the two of us go into a conscious trance we feel a sense of being in a "high-vibration zone" where information seems to flow easily.

Some people report experiencing increased clairvoyance or clairsentience after practicing the art of automatic writing. This has been the case with us as well. The mere willingness to try it will often have the effect of opening oneself up to receiving information from discarnate sources.

As we've said, automatic writing is the method that works best for us, whether we are describing someone's past lives, the present situation, or future events. Try it, and decide if it is a technique that comes easily to you or that you would like to develop.

Channel Surfing

The dictionary defines "channel" as "a means of access, a route." Channeling is a technique whereby one enters a trance state that allows a spirit entity to come through. The channeler then becomes a conduit for information delivered by the spirit. As we've said, meditation is one of the most powerful tools we all have for achieving the kind of mental focus and openness that allow this kind of information to flow. And automatic writing is one of the ways we can receive channeled information.

Linda herself first began channeling in the early eighties in New York City. She felt a spontaneous urge to speak words that were clearly coming from a nonphysical source. She would enter a trance state and begin to speak while Terry took notes. Linda even held channeling sessions for groups of people. Eventually Terry also began to channel and realized that she had a natural capability for it as well.

She would do a meditation and channel answers to Linda's questions. While channeling, we feel more confident, sometimes speaking with more authority and emphasizing certain words or phrases we don't normally use. Sometimes we feel the need to speak very quickly, and with a sense of urgency. We detach from our conscious mind and allow our guides to give us information or messages our client may need to be made aware of. Our channeling is what eventually led to our automatic writing.

When we began doing automatic writing, the language in which we wrote seemed almost archaic in character, as if it were coming from a being who had lived many centuries ago. We knew that our spirit helpers were working through us, but at the time we had no idea of the magnitude of the special gift we had been given.

In the days and months that followed, the two of us became consumed with the process of writing and exploring this new-found gift. If we could receive information about one subject, we wondered, why couldn't we receive information about *any* subject? We practiced predicting for friends on many topics: moving, the purchase of a home, boyfriends coming or going, jobs, and career choices. Soon, people were calling from all over the country for our predictions, which more often than not came to pass. This surprised us as much as it did them, but eventually we came to trust our abilities more and more. As we practiced, we became better at knowing whether the information was coming from a spiritual place—that is, from an entity outside ourselves—or from our unconscious or subconscious minds. Both kinds of wisdom are valuable. We all benefit from becoming conscious of whatever knowledge we may be holding in our subconscious. But that is not the same as receiving information from a spiritual being on a higher plane. Sometimes it just is not possible to know the source of the information, but it never hurts to ask!

CHANNELING LITERARY MASTERPIECES

Some writers use automatic writing as a means of freeing up their thoughts and overcoming writer's block. William Blake said that he wrote his poem "Jerusalem" from "immediate dictation," twelve or sometimes twenty or thirty lines at a time, adding that "I may praise it, since I dare not pretend to be other than the Secretary; the authors are in eternity." And Harriet Beecher Stowe also swore that it was another hand writing through hers when she wrote *Uncle Tom's Cabin*.

A Technique to Practice Automatic Writing

When you do this, be sure that you are in a quiet place where you won't be disturbed for at least an hour. We suggest that you work with a legal pad and a fine-point felt or easy-flowing roller-tip pen.

1. Close your eyes, and breathe deeply and quietly for a few minutes to relax.
2. Say a protection prayer, asking that your channeled information come from the highest place or source of energy. We use this one, but you can use any prayer that feels natural to you: "I generously employ all available loving resources, all guides, angels, beings, and entities of the highest wisdom and vibration. Please surround and protect me, and give me assistance from the highest vibration."
3. Open your eyes and place the point of your pen on your legal pad, making sure that your upper arm is loose and free from the shoulder. Start by drawing large circles, using your entire arm. If you use only your wrist, it will feel too restrictive.
4. Ask your spirit guide a question about himself or herself. Start with a small, simple question. It could be something like: "What is your name? Describe yourself." You may begin to write details about your guide's physical appearance

or clothing. You can also ask your guide why he or she is working with you.

5. Then ask a simple question about something you want to know. It helps to start with a yes or no question such as, "Will I have a romance soon?" or "Will I get a new job?" or "Am I going to take a trip to the lake this summer?"

6. Soon you will feel as if your pen is moving across the pad without your conscious direction. You may write something before you think it. Or you may find yourself doodling symbols or pictures or spiral shapes. Just go with it. If your pen doesn't move at all, try making loopy-loops or circular shapes across the page to start the motion. Call on your guide to help you relax and just start writing whatever thoughts, however mundane, come into your mind. Doing this may help to trigger your hand to begin writing from a higher source without your conscious direction. Another tactic you can use is to change the nature of the question you are asking. Not everyone will have the ability to do automatic writing, but give it a few sessions before deciding the technique isn't for you. You may discover that, after a period of trial and error, you do have an ability to write automatically.

7. Divine messages from spirit resonate deep in your heart. They are often the simplest of answers—sometimes just numbers, dates, or initials. Sometimes the scribbling may be unreadable. After a few sessions, you will find that the words become more legible.

8. Thank your guide for his or her help and count to three to bring yourself out of the session.

After your session, ask yourself these questions to assess the results:

• Did I receive any insights?
• Did the exercise open me up to a solution or a line of thinking that had not occurred to me before?

- Did I make a connection with a loved one in spirit?
- Did words come in that I wouldn't normally use? (Maybe archaic language from another time?)
- Does the scribble look like a picture of something or a symbol?
- Was the answer different from what I would have thought or expected?
- Did this exercise cause me to examine something from a new perspective?

Don't overanalyze your writing or drawings too much. Have deep respect for your own intuitive process, and be patient. You will know they are meaningful when you begin to receive answers to questions you have been curious about—information that resonates on a deep level.

When we were stymied about our various illnesses and needed deeper answers than doctors were giving us, automatic writing became a survival tool, a direct line to spirit. You may want to see if you can get answers about where to live, what career to pursue, what your life purpose is, what healing modality may be most effective, whether a particular college or course of study is positive, and so on. The most common questions our clients ask have to do with love or money. You may want to try automatic writing to get a description of your future partner or the solution to a financial problem. Try not to make the question too complicated. Don't try to find the cure for cancer or solve world hunger in your first attempts, but if, after several sessions, you're still not able to do it, this technique is probably not for you.

Practice with a Partner

Being able to do automatic writing at will takes practice and the ability to detach yourself from conscious thought or ego. Receiving information for yourself is often more difficult than obtaining it for someone else, because when it is about us we are, quite naturally, emotionally attached to the result and may, without being consciously aware of what we're doing, write the answer we want to hear. It may, therefore, be easier to start by practicing automatic writing for another person—which is why it was particularly helpful that there were two of us working when we started. We could team up and each get more objective answers for the other twin. When we teach workshops, we have our students pair off and work in tandem. Choose a friend whom you trust and who has an open mind.

1. Sit in chairs facing each other, with a legal pad and pens. (If the paper is too small, you might feel restricted.)
2. Choose which partner will be the first to ask a question and which person will deliver the message through the writing.
3. The partner who is asking should pose a simple question like "What should I know about my boyfriend?" or "Is my grandmother around me?"
4. The partner doing the writing will start to write out the answer. Sometimes the answers come in the form of images, thoughts, symbols or pictures, phrases, or even childlike scribbles. Don't be surprised if your automatic handwriting is different from your normal writing. After you are finished writing, share with your partner (the questioner) whatever came to you as a thought or in your writing.
5. Now switch places (so that the one writing becomes the questioner and vice versa) and repeat steps 3 and 4.

It is important that you don't second-guess yourself or doubt the validity of whatever may come up. These judgments are ego-based and can block us from receiving higher messages. For example, if your partner is asking about love and you don't trust men, your opinion will color your answer. Ask your angels to remove judgment and criticism from your mind.

It can take some time—sometimes years of practice—to tell the difference between thoughts that come from your own subconscious and those that come from a spirit source, and to trust that you are receiving accurate messages. If it is coming from a higher realm, you will feel centered, safe, and unconditionally loved. The process should feel comforting and uplifting.

Start with short sessions and gradually build up to longer ones. When you begin to feel tired or drained, end the session and clear your energy field by thanking your guides and asking them to help you disconnect from the other person's energy. When you are done, imagine pink rose quartz crystal light flowing through and around you like a waterfall, cleansing your aura. It's always a good idea to wash away any residual energy and renew yourself after making a psychic connection.

If you don't have much success with the writing at first, that's okay. Stay open and aware. Keep practicing. You may find that your strength is in another form of intuition.

Try Automatic Typing

If you would like to practice "automatic typing," you can do so on your computer. Use the method described above to trigger a conscious trance state, ask your question, and gently place your fingers on the keyboard. Call upon your guide and, without editing your thoughts, type whatever comes through.

After a few minutes, you may begin typing more quickly. Don't worry about punctuation or typos. These can be corrected later. You may find it helpful to focus your gaze on an object near the computer, which will distract your left brain while you type. Try not to censor the writing or make sense of it at first. Just stay with it, and be in the flow. It takes some practice, so be patient with yourself. You'll improve with each session.

At first it may feel as though you are just typing your own thoughts, and not those coming from another dimension or from your guide. Keep typing anyway. Eventually you will be able to discern the difference.

We always save our writing (right now we have two file cabinets full) and make sure to note the date at the top of the page so that we will have a record of what came through for us. By keeping these records we are able to go back and check the accuracy of our predictions and potential time frames against actual outcomes. You might want to do this, too, in order to track your progress and the accuracy of the messages you receive.

If you find that automatic writing is not your psychic strong suit, there are many other tools you can try. Read on!

15

Try Psychometry

The term "psychometry," from the Greek words *"psyche"* and *"metric,"* literally means "soul-measuring." It was coined in 1840 by Dr. Joseph Rodes Buchanan, a professor of physiology at the Eclectic Medical Institute in Covington, Kentucky, to refer to information gathered directly from the soul. He believed that thoughts, actions, and events leave impressions on objects and that these impressions can be accessed by someone with psychometric abilities. Then, in the early 1900s, a German physician named Gustav Pagenstecher, who was practicing medicine in Mexico, observed that one of his patients was able to derive visual, olfactory, taste, auditory, and other sensations from objects she held while under hypnosis and could also acquire knowledge of the objects' histories and past associations.

Simply put, psychometry, a kind of clairsentience, is the ability to tune in psychically to the vibrations or energy given off by an object that belongs or belonged to another person in order to receive information about that person or about the history of the object itself. It can be performed using any object: sunglasses, keys, a pendant, a ring, or an item of clothing such as a hat or a shoe. Psychometry is actually a form of scrying—a psychic way of seeing something that is not ordinarily visible to the human eye.

AN EXERCISE TO PRACTICE SCRYING

While psychometry accesses spiritual information by using the sense of touch, scrying is done with a crystal ball, by reading reflections on black glass, the surface of water, or, as in the exercise below, gazing into a flame. Nostradamus, the sixteenth-century French prophet, had visions that he later recorded in verse form while staring into water or fire late at night.

To try accessing this kind of spiritual vision, wait until evening and light a white candle. Be sure that you are in a place where there are no drafts to interfere with the way the candle burns. While staring into the flame, ask a question about a future event. A dim flame signifies that it is advisable to wait before taking action or making a decision. A large, bright flame indicates a favorable outcome. If the flame dances and moves around, there will soon be a change in your plans.

A person who has psychometric abilities could, for example, hold an antique gold ring and be able to identify something about the history of the ring, about the person who owned it, and even the experiences that person had while in possession of the ring. The psychic might be able to sense something of the owner's personality, what they did for a living, and even how the person died. Most important perhaps, an object will often retain the energy of its owner's emotions.

Linda once walked into a New Age store that sold gemstones and crystals, and a display of beautiful stones caught her eye. A young salesman approached her and said, "Aren't they beautiful? This one is from the Maori tribe, the indigenous people of New Zealand." He placed it in Linda's hand. It was a small, polished gray stone with a lavender spiral pattern of shale. Linda held the stone for only a few seconds, but it seemed almost to heat up in her hand. Upon leaving the store, she found that she had lost her voice completely and felt extremely fatigued. There was something very powerful about that stone that seemed to overtake her. However, Linda sensed that it was not a negative energy, but a strong healing energy associated with the previous owner from the Maori tribe. After about thirty minutes, her voice and strength returned.

The two of us attributed this response to the fact that stones can be catalysts for healing. Sometimes the triggered healing is uncomfortable, but there is usually a reason for the response. Linda had lost her voice almost totally for seven years when she was in her twenties, and losing it again now may have been a necessary step in healing her vulnerable throat chakra.

We've used psychometry often in our psychic detective work, because holding an object that belonged to a crime victim or to a suspect can tell us a lot about how, when, and where a crime may have occurred. It can also tell us a good deal about the criminal's personality, age, ethnic background, and even past actions and current situation or location. This is known as "psychic profiling." Using our psychic abilities, we can often determine the criminal's MO, the victim's identity, the weapon used, the degree of abuse or hostility associated with the crime, whether the person who committed the crime has a criminal record, and even predict the perpetrator's future behavior.

One of the most fascinating murder cases we ever worked on involved the mysterious death of a high-ranking officer in the military. We'll call him "Luke." His wife, whom we'll call "Megan," contacted us to get to the bottom of the mystery. Luke's death (by a rifle at close range) was immediately ruled a suicide by the military. The police had closed the case before a complete investigation was conducted and, as a result, Megan had been denied the benefits she would have received if her husband had been murdered. After Megan mailed us photos of the crime scene and an article of his clothing, we tuned in to the energy of the victim's clothing. Using clairsentience and psychometry, we immediately determined that Luke had been murdered. We told Megan there had been a cover-up that went to the highest level of the military, and we suggested that she hire her own private investigator. At our urging, she turned to a renowned forensic pathologist, who flew across the country with a team of four other experts. Luke's body was exhumed, and an autopsy proved that his death could not have been a suicide. The trajectory of the bullet wound proved definitively that this was, in fact, a homicide. Megan ended up seeking the help of the state government to clear her husband's name and finally obtained financial compensation. She called us her angels, and told us, "You were the ones that gave me the hope to get the exhumation and clear my husband's name." We believe that Megan's husband was clearly reaching out from beyond the grave to solve his own murder.

Working with psychometry may trigger visual impressions of people or places, and even facilitate predictions. Not only is it one of the tools most often used in psychic detective work, but it is also a good way for beginning students to start developing their psychic intelligence.

Hone Your Psychometry Skills

Working with a partner, close your eyes and take a few minutes to breathe deeply and put yourself in a meditative state of mind. Open your eyes and ask your partner to give you a piece of jewelry, a watch, a ring, a pair of glasses, an item of clothing, or some other article that's been inherited or acquired. While you're holding the object, see what feelings or thoughts you receive about its history and origin from the residual energy clinging to the object. Ask your guides to help you receive this information. Do not try to control what comes into your mind. The need to control your conscious mind is the main barrier to accessing intuition. To receive spirit-driven intuitive knowledge, you need to bypass the conscious thought process and *allow* a higher way of knowing to come through.

Now, close your eyes again and notice what you see, sense, or hear while holding the object. When Terry first did this exercise in a classroom setting, she held a ring belonging to her partner and accurately described a house on a lake in the woods, trees on the property, her partner's sailboat, and many other details. The more you do it, the more you, too, will glean from holding an inanimate object. Psychometry, as we mentioned, is a form of clairsentience, and people who are clairsentient are particularly good at doing this exercise.

We strongly advise that after doing this exercise you wash your hands with cold water and a bit of salt to cleanse them of any negative energy that might have been clinging to whatever you were holding. This is an effective form of psychic protection.

Use Crystals and Gemstones to Heighten Intuition

Just as feeling the residual energy in an object can help you to receive information about its history and/or its owner, carrying or holding special gems or crystals can help enhance and increase your psychic intelligence. They can serve to open and activate your chakras or energy centers, thereby stimulating the Clairs.

Because crystals and other stones are minerals, they have energy, and the kind of energy they have is specific to the particular kind of stone, which is why different crystals and gemstones are associated with different powers. Some people put them on their forehead (third-eye chakra), while others lie down and surround themselves with crystals to encourage dreams. You may also place them on a part of your body that you wish to heal, or carry them in little pouches every day. Knowledge of which crystals produce which particular energies is a part of ancient wisdom that has been handed down through the centuries. In ancient times and the Middle Ages, most Jews, Christians, and Muslims believed in the protective and healing power of crystal amulets, which were worn on the body to ward off evil or to increase good luck.

Here are a few of the more popular stones and some of the powers associated with them:

- *Amber* is a stone that transmutes negative energy into positive and stimulates the intellect. Wear it to balance mental, physical, and emotional energies.
- *Amethyst* is the stone of contentment. It purifies, encourages healing, and assists in meditation. A good clearing crystal for removing negativity, toxic energy, and fear, this stone also helps in connecting with your guardian angel or guide. It cuts through illusion and enhances psychic ability.
- *Aventurine* can help you attain a promotion or a raise. Be assertive and ask for what you need. This green stone reinforces your decisiveness and leadership abilities.
- *Bloodstone* is good for starting a new business venture or changing jobs. It also reduces stress and is helpful for those who are self-employed.
- *Hematite* is for protection and grounding. This powerful stone will assist in focusing your energy and revitalizing circulation. A strong grounding stone, hematite assists in carrying high-frequency energies while helping you stay connected to the earth.
- *Lapis lazuli* energizes the throat center, enhancing psychic abilities and communication with your spirit guide. The stone of royalty, lapis can help protect the wearer from physical danger or psychic attacks from others. It is also a stone of self-knowledge and reflection that expands awareness and assists in accessing knowledge of past lives.
- *Malachite* is the "transformation stone." It assists you in changing jobs, in handling situations that aren't working, or with clearing blockages on the path to a desired goal.
- *Moonstone*, a calming stone, can be used for protection in traveling. Wear it on the plane and practice breathing deeply if you are anxious about flying. It is also a feminine stone, effective in promoting fertility.
- *Obsidian*, the "mirror stone," can help with forgiveness, releasing grievances, and unconscious emotional blocks. This

stone also increases courage and helps with recovery from trauma.

- *Onyx* banishes grief and deflects the negativity of others.
- *Rose quartz*, another calming stone, is good to wear in a chaotic or crisis situation. It brings powerful energy to healing emotional wounds. Known as the heart stone, rose quartz helps in clearing anger, guilt, shame, fear, and jealousy.

Whether you use them to enhance psychic intelligence, to encourage dreams, or to heal, it is a good idea to run the stones or crystals under cool water or put them in a glass bowl and soak them in very diluted salt water, or a solution of vinegar and water, to cleanse them before and after using them.

If you've ever gone to a thrift shop or a vintage clothing store and picked up an item that gave you a strong feeling—good or bad—you are probably clairsentient and were feeling the energy of the item's former owner. In the following chapter we'll be discussing how you can gain access to the energies of those in spirit more directly—through mediumship.

16

Mediumship—Or, "Mother?...Is That You?"

We believe that the soul survives death. Every living thing is composed of energy and energy never dies, it simply changes form. Therefore, the soul is eternal and continues to exist on another plane after the death of the body. Mediumship is the ability to communicate with the spirits of those who have passed and provide evidence that the soul lives on after physical death. Buddha, Jesus, Muhammad, Moses, and the prophets of the Bible were all mediums in the sense that they brought through wisdom from higher dimensions, teaching us that life does not stop with death. In truth, there are no dead people!

A medium's purpose is not to predict the future, but to communicate with spirits residing on the astral plane and deliver messages that give comfort or closure to those who are grieving the loss of a loved one. As practicing psychic mediums for more than twenty years, we often use automatic writing to bring through messages for our clients from the loved ones they have lost. It is rewarding work because it is so profoundly healing for our clients. Some mediums are clairvoyant and can see spirits; those who are clairaudient hear their messages, and clairsentients tend to sense their presence. Very often, using tarot cards can assist a medium who is particularly clairvoyant to make the link to the spirit realm. Clairaudient mediums find that meditating with music assists them.

Although family members who have passed may sometimes act as spirit guides, most spirits do not come through to give specific guidance such as, "You should buy the house," "Fix the plumbing in the bathroom," or "Move to Zimbabwe." Most often they are there to give a simple message of love. One teacher of ours said that spirits will say as little as they can get away with. It isn't necessarily their purpose to instruct loved ones on earth.

Some people won't make any kind of decision or take any kind of action until they receive a message delivered to them by spirit. This is truly an unhealthy type of dependency. Certainly we want to know that our loved ones are still connected to us, but their job is not to tell us how to live our lives; it's to continue their own soul development on the spiritual plane. In fact, one of the main benefits of connecting with someone in spirit is to create the closure that allows both you and the one in spirit to move on.

You, Too, Can Contact Those in Spirit

Although psychic mediums do act as intermediaries for others, the truth is that anyone *can* receive messages directly from those in spirit, and in this chapter we'll help you discover how to do that. However, as with all the skills we describe and teach, some people will be more adept at this than others. While we all have the ability to sense the presence of those in spirit and to communicate with them, becoming a medium and bringing in messages for others is a special talent you may or may not have. And we often find that even those who do have this ability have neglected it or suppressed it so long that they don't realize they have it.

Your loved ones in spirit do want to communicate with you (and may actually be sending you messages you're simply not noticing). But a medium can't just "dig up" someone else's loved one at will. It's always up to the spirits to decide whether or not they will come through.

We once took a weeklong workshop with mediums from the Arthur Findlay College at Stansted in England, and as part of the program Linda was called upon to do an exercise that involved mediumship. She felt an icy chill come over her, and she was compelled to take five or six steps backward, as if some force was gently propelling her, until she was standing next to one of our instructors, Nora Shaw. (Nora later explained to the class that it is common to experience a temperature change or a chill when one is in the presence of a deceased spirit.)

At that point Linda said, "An older man is coming in who calls himself Alexander. He has little wire-rimmed spectacles and salt-and-pepper hair. He is telling me he was a student of yours some years ago." Nora nodded in acknowledgment. "Go on," she encouraged. Linda continued, saying, "Alexander comes to you with so much reverence and love. You were his favorite teacher, and he loved you so very much." Nora was clearly touched, but she tried to remain neutral as Linda channeled her friend. "He misses you, but he will see you again. He wants you to know he is an angel for you." Nora smiled, her eyes brimming with tears, and said, "Very good, Linda. No one has ever brought my friend Alexander through before—not even me. He was one of my best students. I have been waiting to hear from him for years. Thank you so much."

Not everyone is destined to become the next American Idol of mediumship. The best advice we can give is not to compare yourself to others. Mediumship is a very personal and powerful art. Just try to do your best, and you will improve naturally over time as you find your own style and rhythm. Once again, be patient with yourself! If you are open and receptive when practicing mediumship, the world of spirit will almost certainly reveal itself to you. Still, we have encountered some people who, despite a strong desire and willingness, simply don't have an aptitude for mediumship. If that turns out to be the case for you, trust that your strengths will lie elsewhere—perhaps in precognition, receiving messages through dreams, or as an intuitive healer.

A NATIVE AMERICAN PRAYER

This is the poem we recited at our mother's funeral. It's one of our favorites because death, to us, is not an end. It is a new beginning. We still feel connected to our loved ones in spirit, and their communication with us continues from the other side. Our mother loved nature, and we feel her in the beauty of nature all around us: in gardens, birds, the change of seasons. Although our relationship with her was not always an easy one, we welcome the connection with her, and we feel at peace when we read this poem.

I give you this
One thought to keep.
I am with you still
I do not sleep.

I am a thousand winds that blow.
I am the diamond glints in snow.
I am the sunlight on ripened grain,
I am the gentle autumn rain.

When you awaken
In the morning's hush
I am the swift uplifting rush
Of quiet birds in circled flight.
I am the soft stars
That shine at night.

Do not think of me as gone—
I am with you still
In each new dawn.

How Mediums Receive Their Messages

Messages from those in spirit come through the same channels as any other forms of psychic intelligence. A medium can receive messages through psychic hearing (clairaudience), or "see" symbols and imagery pertaining to a significant characteristic or event (clairvoyance). This might include physical appearance, facial features, clothing, a particular hairstyle or hair color, and if the person wore glasses or jewelry. Numbers, dates, colors, a certain phrase, or a particular way of walking or talking can also come through with vivid accuracy. And through clairsentience a medium can sometimes get a "feel" for how a person passed or perhaps for a health condition that was troubling to him or her in life. For example, the two of us sometimes feel a pain in the back if the person had a back problem. The sudden onset of a headache may indicate a head injury or illness suffered by the deceased.

Although the two of us use all our Clairs when we do mediumship, we most often receive information through our automatic writing and claircognizance. How you receive messages will certainly depend upon which of your own Clairs is the strongest.

Honor Your Gift

Before you attempt to contact anyone in spirit, it's important that you protect yourself from any possible negative energy that might come through. To do this, we recommend you follow one of the protective rituals described on pages 57–58, or simply ask your spirit guides for protection.

Don't do this for the fun of it. Mediumship is not a parlor game and should be practiced with great reverence. It is a sacred office, and we must respect ourselves as well as the gift. All information related must be kept in the greatest confidence, not unlike a confession made in church. Perhaps for this reason, mediums rarely remember the information they receive during a mediumship session.

If you are doing this for another person, make a contract of intent, which is a sort of mission statement and might be something like, "I dedicate myself to this work to help others." We've noticed that our clients don't always remember exactly what we told them, but they do remember how we made them feel—happier and lighter—and many also report having a great sense of closure. For that reason, it is important to come from a place of compassion and love rather than from a place of ego. Any work that involves compassion, such as healing, counseling, and mediumship, will stimulate your empathy, and therefore your psychic ability.

And again, it is also extremely important that you never try to control or manipulate others while doing this work. When engaging in mediumship, try not to tell people what to do—such as whether or not they should leave a marriage, quit their job, or make some other type of life-changing decision. Everyone has free will and must be allowed to make his or her own choices. Some psychics will actually say, "Your aunt Bernice is telling you to invest your money in a certain piece of land." Or, "Your wife is coming to me with a message that you need to leave your new girlfriend. She's bad for you." We do not condone this, and we believe that it can be unethical and harmful to work this way. Mediumship is an art that should be approached with the utmost integrity.

We agree completely with the famous medium James Van Praagh, who warns against using one's psychic powers for ego or personal gain, or to control other people. This falls under the category of psychic ethics and responsibility, and we have always been careful not to tell people how to live their lives unless they are actually in a life-threatening situation.

Unfortunately, there is no governing authority to oversee the ethical behavior of psychics and mediums. The two of us have had many people come to us with horrifying stories of abuse by professional "psychics." We think that psychics should function by the same Hippocratic oath as doctors: First, do no harm.

One of our clients (we'll call her "Gayle") became very emotional as she told us about having been approached in a hair salon by a woman wielding a blow-dryer. She had all the subtlety of an armored tank.

"Your husband is addicted to porn!" she warned. "It's under the bed behind a suitcase near the wall. I am a psychic and I have to tell you—he has also been cheating on you!"

Gayle could not believe what she was hearing, and, even worse, her young daughter was standing right there next to her. As it turned out, the hairdresser was correct—there was a stash of pornographic videos exactly where she had said, and Gayle later discovered text messages revealing his affair. But the hairdresser's revelation was totally unsolicited, and it came like a "guerrilla psychic attack" out of left field. Gayle was shaken for years afterward, and even now continues to be haunted by the memory.

It is almost always inappropriate to deliver psychic messages that haven't been requested. And it is always necessary to think before you speak. Some people are simply not ready for the information or message you may have for them, and they certainly don't deserve to be clobbered over the head unexpectedly.

Let Go of Your Doubts

If you're doubtful of your ability to contact those in spirit, there is probably some long-held, possibly subconscious belief you've been harboring or a message you were given at some time in the past that's preventing you from believing in yourself. To rid yourself of those negative messages and beliefs, get out your journal and ask yourself the following questions:

- What do I believe about connecting with loved ones on the other side?
- Do I believe it is even possible to communicate with those who have passed?
- What am I afraid of?

- Am I afraid I will start seeing scary dead people like on TV and in movies?
- What did my family teach me to believe about death?
- What do my religious beliefs teach me about death?
- Are there unresolved issues such as a childhood trauma, betrayal by a parent or loved one, abandonment or victimization, or other forms of abuse I need to heal first?
- Am I upset or traumatized for any reason by the passing of a loved one?
- Am I holding on to feelings of anger toward someone who has passed?
- Am I angry with myself? With the one who has passed? Why?
- Whom do I need to forgive—myself, the other person, both?

Now write a positive affirmation or sentence to contradict each fear. Call upon your angels to help you form the best affirmation. For example, if you answered the third point "I am afraid of death," your affirmation would be "I am safe, and I trust that dying is a natural process. I will have all the assistance I need."

Here are a few of the kinds of feelings that commonly prevent people from exploring their ability to make psychic connections with those in spirit, along with affirmations you can say to dispel your fears:

- *Feeling:* I am afraid I will see scary ghosts like in the horror movies.

  Affirmation: Hollywood movies are fiction, and spirits cannot harm me. I am safe and protected always. My loved ones are in a beautiful, safe place.
- *Feeling:* My family taught me to fear death.

  Affirmation: Dying is a natural part of life, and I do not need to take on the fears or beliefs of my family members.
- *Feeling:* I am still angry with [name a family member or friend] for leaving me when I was so young.

Affirmation: I accept that it was their time to go, and they're happy now.

- *Feeling:* I am angry with myself for not being able to save [name the person whose passing you were unable to prevent].

  Affirmation: I forgive myself and give myself a break. It is not possible for me to rescue anyone if it is that person's time to cross over.

To Get Started: Attunement

To connect with a friend or loved one in spirit, begin to think about the person with whom you would like to connect. This process will allow your thoughts and emotions to float up from your subconscious mind and become more present for you. Get out your journal and write down the following:

- Name one person in spirit with whom you most want to connect.
- Describe what your relationship with this person was like in life.
- What was the person like? Funny? Serious? Eccentric? Difficult?
- What were the person's interests? Passions? Dreams?
- Describe this person's personality.
- What one thing do you remember most fondly about this person?
- Why do you want to make a connection with this person?
- What do you expect to hear, feel, or see?
- If it is a parent you want to connect with, were you the favorite child? An only child? Neglected? Spoiled?
- If it is a sibling, did your parents treat them as though they were more important than you? Less important? How did that make you feel?
- Would you consider this person more or less successful than you?

When you are trying to make the connection, let go of any expectations you may have of who will come through and how a particular individual will come through for you. You may be disappointed if you think that they will talk about something specific that happened in your past. For example: "My mother had better tell me where she hid the family money," or "Uncle Tony needs to apologize for getting drunk at my wedding." Try to be open to whatever thoughts, messages, or impressions may come in.

If you do not get a message from a loved one, it may be because you are not ready for it. You may need to heal your anger, fear, or grief issues before a connection is possible. Consider joining a bereavement group or seeing a grief counselor, even if it is only for a short time. Remember, your loved ones in spirit always want to make the connection with you. Why would you block it? Go back to the list of doubts or misconceptions you might have about death and/or contacting those who have passed. You may be unconsciously blocking communication without even realizing that you are! While we may not be able to control the messages we receive or how they come through, we can work on opening our own mind. Through patience and practice, we can develop our muscles of mediumship in much the same way a bodybuilder develops his physical muscles. Are you willing to give yourself the time to do that?

And when you do receive a message, trust that you are not making it up. It is not coming from you. Know that it is true. We're not saying it's always easy to do that; in fact, it took us many years to trust the messages we were receiving. As you develop your four Clairs, you will begin to trust more, and the messages or signs will come in with greater clarity and consistency. For instance, you may see a hummingbird at the same time every day or at a particularly important time. You may hear a song that was your mother's favorite, or the music your father played when he danced with you. Two good affirmations for developing trust would be: "I trust that the spirit messages are true and pure," and "I trust my psychic gift to connect with spirit."

TUNE IN TO THE HIGHER FREQUENCY

Spirits vibrate at a different rate than we do on the earth plane, because they are literally on a different dimension. It is a finer, faster vibration than ours, and we have to raise our own vibration to access the voices of spirit beings. This is known as "attunement." For us, tuning in is very similar to turning on a radio and changing stations. Over the years, we have refined our psychic instrument so that we trust the information we are receiving from higher realms. It is important to learn how to translate your intuitive ideas into language. As you refine your vibration, you will learn to speak words that express what you are seeing and hearing in a clear yet evocative and inspiring way. Ask your spirit guides to help you develop your communication skills. Educating yourself on various subjects is important in doing readings for others. Reading books and writing poetry or journaling will help you with this. The more knowledge you have in general and the greater your vocabulary, the more information the spirit will have to work with.

With practice, you, too, can develop a subtle vocabulary of words, imagery, and concepts for interpreting the symbols and messages you receive in a way that will resonate with the person for whom you are reading. You will gradually learn to articulate subtle feelings or impressions coming through from the person in spirit.

Here is an exercise you can do to raise your vibration:

1. Close your eyes and imagine a white, gold, or silver light glowing within your abdomen. White is the color of spirituality, gold is the color of inspiration, and both gold and silver are the colors of protection.
2. Expand this light to fill your body.
3. Expand the light to surround your body and embrace everyone else in the room.
4. When you see yourself as being filled with light, you will become more connected to the wisdom of spiritual energy.

Making the Connection

Overanalyzing or thinking too much can interfere with the flow of intuition. You may have heard the expression "When the student is ready, the teacher will appear," and the same can be said of spirits. Mediumship is reaching to a higher dimension; it is a gift.

Mentally, you will be asking questions of the spirit. Some examples of the information you can ask to receive:

- Name of the spirit
- Physical description
- Occupation
- Relationship (i.e., you may receive feelings that are motherly, or playful and childlike)
- Manner of death, such as an illness or accident, including symptoms you may feel in your own body
- Temperament (i.e., whether the person was blustery, calm, nervous, bossy, nosy, or a prankster in their physical life)
- Shared memories or anecdotes
- Special dates
- Specific messages

At first, when you ask for information you will truly feel as if you are making up or imagining whatever you receive. Don't push the information away. Don't doubt the impression you are getting in the moment; just go with it. To constantly doubt is like driving a car with the brakes on. Know that the one in spirit really wants to come through to convey a loving message.

Over time, you will begin to trust your abilities more, and start to relax.

When You Are Serving as the Medium for Another Person

First, Prepare the Room

Make sure that it is clean and that the light isn't too bright. Set up the room so that you and the person for whom you are making the connection have a comfortable place to sit. Place fresh drinking water and tissues within easy reach. Place a lit candle and fresh greens or flowers on a table.

Help the Sitter Feel at Ease

Ask if this is their first reading. Explain clearly what they can expect, and do your best to alleviate their fears. You may want to say that whoever comes in may be different from the person they want to contact.

During one lecture at the Learning Annex we were bringing through a message from a woman's husband. "Oh, I don't give a damn about him!" was her immediate response, causing the rest of the audience to burst out laughing. Remind your sitters that you can't control who comes through (it will usually be the spirit or spirits with the strongest and most dynamic personality), and that they might not necessarily be happy to hear from those who do.

Establish the Connection

Ask the same questions we suggested that you ask when making a connection for yourself (page 181). Begin by establishing if this is a friend or relative. What is the relationship? Ask the spirit for a message, a description, or an area of interest. You may ask how the spirit passed, or if there was a long or short illness. While many mediums do not ask for specific names, we are especially good at getting names. In fact, we sometimes get ten to twenty or more names the client will recognize. Sometimes the sitter will verify a name later by checking with a relative or consulting the family genealogy. One client called after a session to accuse us of Googling her entire ancestry because she simply could not believe we were receiving the names of all her loved ones with such accuracy!

We encourage the beginning medium to ask specifically for a healing message of comfort for the sitter. It doesn't have to be the Psychic Olympics, with a high degree of difficulty. Start with baby steps. Even the simplest message can bring tremendous comfort to someone in pain. "I don't blame you for what happened," or "I am sorry for not being there for you as a child" are simple communications that may be very healing. We have seen mediums describe red shoes under the bed or a photograph on the bedside table—details that contain no message of comfort or solace for those waiting in grief. This is why we stress that empathy and compassion are such important qualities for a medium to develop.

It may be difficult, particularly if you are a beginner, to remain calm and distance yourself from all the emotions in the room. If you feel you are becoming too emotionally involved and/or start to cry, it is a good idea to close your eyes and imagine yourself taking a step back from the spirit coming through. By doing that you are putting a bit of distance between yourself and the spirit so that you are better able to deliver the messages you receive without being overcome by emotion. It took us awhile to master this.

Help Them Understand

Explain that many people become forgetful in this type of situation. Some may even forget their mother's name! Suggest that those who are receiving readings take notes or jot names on a notepad. Many people record the sessions.

Some traditional teachings advise you to give a message and always ask, "Do you understand this?" but this seems too mechanical and artificial to us. With practice, you will find your own appropriate style and wording. When someone comes through, substantiate that the sitter knows who the spirit is and what their relationship was. You might even find yourself limping or speaking with an unfamiliar accent, as it is common for the medium to take on a particular characteristic of the spirit who is coming through. This is a form of evidence that you are making a "link" or psychic connection.

Being a medium is a special gift that is worth developing! As you practice and expand your gift, you will find that you are also growing personally and emotionally in ways you never expected. You will become a more sensitive and compassionate human being. You will stretch past the limits of what you believed was possible. The practice of mediumship not only helps you embrace and come to terms with the process of death, it also teaches you that we all, indeed, survive death. You will learn to become more trusting—of yourself and your spirit helpers. In the process, you will also learn to listen, focus, and pay attention to signs and messages you otherwise might have missed. In centering yourself and going within, you may find that you are able to create a more spiritual and relaxed way of being in the world. You may be inspired to live with less stress, a different set of goals, or new priorities, such as spending more time with your family. Perhaps most important, you will certainly learn more about the unseen dimensions of thought, space, and time... and the world beyond this one.

PART IV

PUT YOUR POWERS TO WORK

The point of acquiring any kind of knowledge is to improve your life. That's really what honing your psychic intelligence is all about. In the following chapters we'll be talking about how you can use what you've learned to make better decisions, to be more productive and fulfilled, and to become your best, most authentic self.

17

Use Your Powers to Enhance Your Life

U sing your psychic intelligence means listening to your inner
voice. That voice whispering in your ear can be your wisest
adviser when it comes to making any kind of important decision. If
you are only open to hearing it and willing to believe what it's telling
you, your inner voice will help you to improve your relationships,
advance your career, create more wealth, and—most important—
discover your true passion and live a more authentic life.

Become a Better Judge of Character

You can use your inner voice to learn more about all the people in
your life—friends, relatives, coworkers, employees, potential romantic partners, and so on. Ask yourself: "Are they people of high integrity and good character? Do they do what they say they will? Am I
compatible with them? Are they respectful of me and of others? Will
they be reliable? Cooperative or difficult? Rebellious or team players? Self-motivating or followers?"

People are constantly giving us verbal and nonverbal cues that
will help us make better decisions about whether or not to pursue
or continue a relationship with a friend, a lover, a business partner,

or even a family member. The problem is that many of us don't pay attention and would rather live in denial than confront the truth about someone else. Your psychic intelligence can help you intuitively address the red flags you were not willing to see in the past, and take constructive action to heal the situation.

How do you do this? Stop, look, listen, feel, know—access your Clairs! Ask the questions above while you are in your morning meditation. Focus on a specific individual and ask the questions to which you seek answers. Call in your angels and guides and the wise counsel of your own intuition. Notice the subtle clues and thoughts that come in. Pay attention to how your body feels. Is it light? Heavy? Tense anywhere? Do you get a sudden feeling of depression or rage? Notice if there is a good feeling or a bad feeling when you focus on this individual, and try to shine a light on that feeling.

CAN YOU TELL WHEN SOMEONE IS LYING?

When we made our second appearance on *The Tyra Banks Show*, we were asked to be psychic lie detectors. Various couples were brought onto the stage and we were sequestered where we could not hear the conversation. It was up to us to decide if the husband or wife was lying about having an extramarital affair. You may be able to trick a lie detector machine, but you can't fool the Psychic Twins!

People send all kinds of verbal and nonverbal signals when they're lying. They may start talking nonstop, pause or stumble, maybe try to change the subject. They may keep repeating a phrase or speak in a monotone. The common denominator is the theme of concealment. Police personnel are trained to ask the right questions and to look for particular body language in order to determine whether a suspect is lying. And a mother can usually tell when her children are lying to her— it's what mothers do! We just have to learn what to look and listen for, and then make sure we're tuned in.

- **Changes in Body Language:** When people are lying they tend either to use much bigger, more dramatic gestures than normal or to try to sit absolutely still, as if almost frozen. Dishonest people may cross their arms in front of their chest defensively, so they feel less "exposed."

- **Changes in Vocal Pitch and Speech Rhythms:** If people start to screech or speak in a high-pitched tone, they may be desperate to convince you of something. They may be protesting their innocence too strongly. And if they're pausing for an unusually long time between words, it may be that they're making it up as they go along—and trying to make it sound really good. Tune in with your psychic inner ear to these kinds of vocal changes. Murderers will often have a very controlled, monotone quality to their voice when fabricating a false alibi. The average person tends to speak with real emotion about a traumatic event, while a liar may sound emotionless or robotic.

- **Eye Contact:** We've all heard the line "Look me in the eye and tell me you're not lying." It's hard to lie when you're making eye contact, so glancing away or not making eye contact at all can be a dead giveaway. But some people will make it a point to stare straight into your eyes while they're lying simply because they think that will make their lie more believable. Either extreme is unnatural. Your intuition can help you decide whether the person avoiding your eyes or staring into your eyes with a hypnotic gaze is telling the truth or selling a lie.

- **Making Nervous Gestures:** You know when the people you're with seem nervous. They may be blinking, fidgeting, rubbing or scratching, clearing their throat, swallowing between words, or covering their mouth while they talk—you know the signs. Or they may turn their body away from you as they're speaking. Maybe that just means they're nervous about how you're going to react to what they have to say. They're worried that you might be angry or disappointed. But maybe it's because they're lying and wondering whether you're going to buy into the lie. Listen to your inner voice—your built-in lie detector—to help you determine what's really going on.

- **Looking Too Innocent:** You know how little kids can look as if butter wouldn't melt in their mouths while they tell you the biggest fib in the world? Well, grown-ups can do that, too. Be aware—and wary—when someone looks like a five-year-old claiming it was their sister who wrote with crayon on the wall. They're probably lying.

Recognize Opportunities When They Present Themselves

If you are unemployed, your intuition can lead you to the right job at the right time, or at least to the right place to look. Maybe there's a little voice in your head telling you to send a résumé or make a cold call to a person or a company with whom you have no personal or professional connection. Instead of dismissing it as a dumb idea, follow your inner voice and just do it. It's possible, of course, that you might be dismissed or rejected, but, as the old saying goes, "Nothing ventured, nothing gained." And more often than not you'll be surprised by the positive response you receive.

Often our most powerful intuitive impressions will have nothing to do with what we're consciously focusing on and will seem to come totally out of the blue. For example, Linda's intuition guided her to send a letter to the producers of *The Tyra Banks Show,* and, much to our surprise, a producer responded with great interest. As a result we appeared on the show twice and drew a huge and positive audience response.

In another instance, ten years ago Terry had just gotten a new computer and, out of nowhere, had a sudden hunch to research opportunities for us to be booked on a cruise ship. We were gobsmacked when we got an enthusiastic response to Terry's query from two women who booked psychic mediums as cruise speakers. We were hired to lecture on the gigantic *Norwegian Sky* as it sailed through the Caribbean. Other speakers on this grand ship were legendary medium Suzane Northrop, star of OUTtv; therapist Edy Nathan, one of the hosts of *Psychic Kids*; and renowned medium John Holland. All of them became our longtime friends, and John later recommended us for a documentary film. None of these events would have unfolded if Terry had not trusted her intuition and followed a hunch.

Using your intuition makes it much easier to be discerning and zero-in on exactly what you want or need. Opportunities are all around us all the time. If you think that other people are always "luckier" than you because good things just seem to drop into their lap, it's probably because they're making it a practice to tune in to their intuitive voice and act on it. When we use our psychic intelligence, we make our own good luck.

Make Better Decisions

Psychic intelligence is your most powerful decision-making tool. If you need to make a split-second decision about how to handle an emergency such as caring for a sick child, or what to do when a stranger is following you on a deserted street, accessing your intuition will show you the way. Personal trainer and former football player Nick Schuyler, whose three friends died when their boat capsized off the Florida coast, attributes his survival to having decided to put on a life jacket *before* the boat capsized. His inner voice let him know that he needed to protect himself, and heeding that psychic whisper in his ear saved his life.

Doctors use intuition along with medical knowledge when diagnosing illnesses and prescribing medications, and businesspeople depend on instinct along with market research to define their target market and develop the best sales strategies. While we're not suggesting that you neglect or ignore academic training or doing factual research, you, too, can use your intuition to enhance and make the best use of any other kind of knowledge you might have or acquire.

A JOURNALING EXERCISE FOR PSYCHIC DECISION MAKING

TV shows and movies about psychics play up the Hollywood special effects, overdramatizing the spooky and weird aspect of psychic experiences to such an extent that people come to think that is what all psychic experiences are like. Not so! Impressions can be quite subtle and abstract, a subliminal inner prompting to avoid a certain street, a nudge by spirit to reach for a certain book on the shelf only to find that it contains just the information you were looking for. Merely setting the intention to open up your receivership or awareness can put the process in motion. Open your journal to a blank page and close your eyes for a few moments. Then focus on a specific choice you need to make.

1. Take some deep breaths and try to let go of any inhibitions, limiting beliefs, and self-doubt that may come up for you. This will help you be more in a place of receptivity and openness so that solutions and guidance may come more easily. Put yourself in the right relationship with your intentions.
2. What is the decision at hand? Write a brief description.
3. What are your immediate feelings about it? Notice any physical sensations such as tightening in the stomach, shallow breathing, or tensing of the jaw or shoulder muscles. Notice also any emotional impressions that may come up, such as anger, resentment, excitement, anxiety, fear, panic, or shame. Record these impressions in your journal.
4. Do you have a sense of expansion or limitation connected with the decision? Try to get a feeling of this in your body. Does a part of your body feel tight, clenched? Is there pain, and if so, where? Does this feeling remind you of a past experience you had where you felt thwarted? Empowered? Write it down.

5. Do you hear thoughts or warnings, a cautionary voice connected with this decision? Write them down even if they don't make sense. They may make sense to you later.

6. Record any feelings that may come up at random during this exercise, trying not to judge them. Negative feelings such as dread, fear, fatigue, or anxiety indicate that you should pay heed and take caution; this may not be your best option. Or you may feel joy, exhilaration, or anticipation, indicating that you are on the right track and getting closer to making the right decision for you. The right decision will almost always bring you a positive feeling such as happiness, enthusiasm, or a feeling of peace or calm. It will feel "right."

7. Ask for clarification: "What should I know about this decision that I don't know yet? What is the most positive direction for me right now? Is there something positive I need to learn from this experience?"

8. Make a clear and decisive choice in your mind and write it down. You can always change it later.

9. Write down your perceptions about the decision you made. Does it feel good to you? What influenced your choice? Did you have positive intentions for the outcome? Did you make the decision out of fear, or from a place of confidence? Is the decision in alignment with your overarching goals? Are you trusting yourself, or are you making this choice to please someone else such as a parent or spouse? Are you beginning to develop a more refined listening, or tuning in, to your psychic impressions?

Predict Possible Outcomes

We have a knack for predicting major news headlines weeks, months, or even years in advance of their happening. A few years ago we made the rounds of network executives pitching a weekly TV news program called *Ahead-line News* to be anchored by the world's top intuitives. The premise was that "any television news show can give you the news after it's happened. But only one news show gives you the news *before* it happens."

The point we want to make here is that people who are out of touch with their psychic intelligence tend to make off-the-cuff decisions that turn out badly because they are not intuiting the possible outcomes. Or, conversely, they may think so much about what *might* happen that they become paralyzed with indecision.

Your intuition will help you predict the outcome of all kinds of important decisions, from the best place to move to finding the best school for your child. You can develop the ability to predict outcomes of anything from health issues to relationships. Your ability to tune in can protect you from making bad business investments, or becoming involved with a shady travel agent.

We once visited a friend who had just moved to a beautiful new home in Seattle. We said, "This is a beautiful place, Laura, but you may not be here long." We told her there might be a fire, and she looked at us like we were two scoops of crazy. Less than a year later, however, she called to tell us we were right. Her kitchen had caught fire and she had to move to a condo!

Another time, we both had a very strong feeling of foreboding when a client named Robyn told us she was selling everything and moving to the East Coast because she had been offered an administrative job. Even though she was convinced it would be good for her, we warned her about moving before all the details of her employment had been worked out.

But Robyn remained stoic in her decision. And, sure enough, she called us from Washington, D.C., in tears. The job had fallen through, and she was up a creek without a paddle because she had sold her furniture and belongings—even her car!

Or what if you're thinking about putting your child in a particular school or program, and you want to know which one will be the best fit. Our friend Dana struggled with this for years, taking her daughter out of one school after another because of personality conflicts with the other students and difficult teachers. Although Dana is naturally intuitive, she often panicked and let her anxieties and fears block her innate psychic intelligence. Because she never took the time to tune in, her fears invariably escalated, alienating the teachers and other parents, and her daughter was the one who paid the ultimate price.

Define or Refine Your Career Goals

Two years ago a man (we'll call him "Ian") came to us because he didn't know what to do or which way to turn in this unpredictable economy. We told him that we saw alternative energy in his life, and in particular, that a biofuel opportunity would soon be coming his way. We suggested that he meditate and visualize the perfect job in which he could create value for himself and the world. Not long ago, we heard from Ian again. He'd been contacted with a lucrative offer from an alternative energy company. Ian jumped at the chance (as we'd told him he should) and has greatly increased his income while doing something he is proud of—helping the environment.

We are constantly getting calls from people who are having trouble defining their career path or students who are confused about choosing the right major. We help them go with their strengths and passions, as well as the latest job trends. We assist them to map out the best program of study or to focus on where the greatest hiring potential might be down the road. This is especially important nowadays, when the job market is so tight and a line of work that was booming five years ago may now be a dead-end endeavor.

To do this for yourself, begin by taking an inventory. Ask yourself: "What is the best way to create value, or make a unique contribution in my work? What is my unique gift?"

What are you good at? What do you enjoy doing?

Do you have a green thumb like Martha Stewart, or can you whip up six different meals in thirty minutes like Rachael Ray? Maybe you could start a catering business from your home. Perhaps you are clever with your hands and have skills with sewing, carving, or refinishing furniture. You might consider home decor or carpentry as possible career paths. Are you good at leading others in exercise? You could be a physical trainer or a Pilates instructor. Maybe you are talented at giving advice to groups of people or training individuals. You could be a coach, tutor, or mentor, empowering others to reach their goals. If you are a good cheerleader, you could be a natural motivator or speaker. Maybe you are good with older people; if so, consider nursing, home care for the sick, or working as an activity coordinator for seniors. As baby boomers age by the millions, this is becoming one of the fastest-growing industries around.

Is your talent gourmet baking, bookkeeping, event planning, repairing appliances? You could turn any of these into bankable skills. If you've raised children, chances are you have many management and teaching skills you could draw on to run your own business or to manage someone else's. If you love to travel, you might consider becoming a travel agent or even a travel writer. Do friends constantly comment on your flair for decorating? This may be a potential small business for you.

You should also make a list of things you truly dislike. Do you hate working in the city? Is an office environment stifling for you? Do you hate following orders? Does a nine-to-five job make you feel like screaming and tearing out your hair? Does the idea of working with people with illnesses scare you? Do you hate housework? Do you avoid cooking like the plague? Does the idea of selling a product make you feel that you'd be taking advantage of people? Knowing what you *don't* want to do will help to point you in the direction of what you do want to do.

Then focus on your weaknesses. You need to be really honest here. Are you disorganized? Are you lousy at money management? Are you dyslexic? Do you spell like a fifth-grader? Are you rebellious or resistant to taking direction from authority figures?

Write it all down. Then meditate on your list every day, and ask your guides to lead you to the place where you will love going to work. Determine that you will find a job you really enjoy and in which you can grow and thrive. Really get the visual and emotional sense of where you want to be. How does your dream job (college, course, vocation) feel in your body? Imagine as vividly as you can the feeling of going to work at your new job and enjoying wonderful, uplifting interactions with your new boss and coworkers.

An intuitive friend of ours had been in an unfulfilling marriage for more than twenty years when she finally divorced her husband and pursued her dream of writing. A Hollywood producer approached her on Facebook to consult for a psychic TV show he was putting together, and she is now a successful Hollywood producer in her own right.

Even if it takes awhile to find your dream job, you never know where you might meet someone to assist you in getting to the next rung on the ladder. Terry once took a reception job for a very high-profile dentist. It was dreary work, but one of the patients told her about an office management position that was opening up, and Terry wound up running a Chinese acupuncture center in Santa Monica for two years. So, don't rule out the power of menial or entry-level jobs.

When you are pursuing a career path, the most important step is to discover what truly makes your heart sing. While many motivational programs cheer you on, telling you, "Go for it!" the biggest problem we find is that people have no idea what they are going *for*. They may be foggy on what their passions are or they may never really have thought about how to develop the passions they have and set goals. When you find what you love and can express yourself through the work you love doing, not only you but also everyone around you will benefit.

Once you've figured out what that is, listen to your inner voice and don't let anyone dampen your dream. When people tell you it can't be done, don't listen. It's your dream—not theirs. Politely say thanks, and ignore them. We know this only too well.

Sharpen Your Financial Smarts

We often think that if all those unfortunate people who turned over their life savings to the financial villain Bernie Madoff had trusted their own intuition, they might have thought twice about what they were doing—and saved both their money and their financial futures.

Some of the smartest people—including scientists and graduates of the most elite business colleges in the world—are actually the most gullible, because they arrogantly assume they cannot be fooled. It's an ego thing. For example, Stephen Greenspan, a University of Colorado professor, wrote a book called *Annals of Gullibility: Why We Get Duped and How to Avoid It*, about how to avoid being conned. The day his book was released, Greenspan learned that he had lost $400,000 of his retirement savings in the Bernie Madoff scam, the largest Ponzi scheme in history. His wife, who had tried in vain to talk him out of investing their nest egg with Madoff because she had a "bad feeling about it," got to have the last word: "I told you so."

For some reason, when it comes to trusting con artists like Madoff with our money, we throw our instincts and caution to the wind. We trust anyone who calls himself a financial counselor or a broker without checking in with our inner wisdom or higher guidance. Why? Because we've been told that we don't know enough to make these decisions for ourselves and we need to rely on the "experts."

Do your own research. If you don't understand an investment or contract, don't do it. More important, tune in to see what your gut feeling is about an investment opportunity. What are your Clairs telling you? More often than not, if it sounds "too good to be true," it probably is. Many of the best-selling books on money, investing, and "getting rich" talk about courage, smarts, and knowledge. Few even mention intuition, which is perhaps the most crucial component. Don't ignore it.

Get the Edge in Business Situations

Now that the job market is supercompetitive, you can tap into your psychic intelligence to get the job you've been searching for. Don't waste time interviewing with the wrong companies or taking the wrong career path. Let your Clairs be your guide.

When we first started out in New York City in the eighties, we began as entertainers in the event market. At that time the best shows you could get for large events were magicians pulling rabbits out of hats, cheesy comics, strippers, and the occasional chimp on roller skates. We noticed very quickly a tremendous lack of creativity and innovation in the corporate event and entertainment market and we knew we could fill the void. Together, we had a truly clairvoyant vision of how to create a new kind of theater that was more like an elegant, otherworldly circus. We saw it all in our mind's eye, and wound up transforming the party market at that time by offering unique and unusual customized themed events to high-end clients such as the White House, the Plaza Hotel, the elegant Hotel Pierre, and many Atlantic City casinos. We provided improvisational comedy, ten-foot-tall stilt dancers, fire-eaters, and trapeze artists, and dressed them in elaborate outsize costumes long before Cirque du Soleil ever existed! The two of us headed our own theatrical troupe, Pop Theatrics—a futuristic fantasy world that delighted and astonished our audiences. Linda designed and constructed most of the costumes with her then-boyfriend, while Terry handled most of the business end of the operations. In addition, we produced, managed, and performed at every party, changing characters and costumes several times throughout the evening. Our audiences were mesmerized, and we took our vision-made-reality up and down the East Coast. We were vogue-ing long before Madonna!

The key to being successful in business is finding out what a company or employer is looking for, and fulfilling that need. Do due diligence and find out what the company needs or values. Begin to brainstorm solutions. Meditate and take the "psychic" pulse of your client or employer. Ask yourself, "What do they need or value? What are they missing, and how can I supply the missing piece? What will this look or feel like?" Jot down the answers that come to you even if they do not make sense at the time. Read them over, then make a list of all your skills, talents, and abilities. It helps to pay attention to the images and ideas that come to you in dreams, as we spoke about in Chapter Thirteen.

You may want to write a mission statement, as we did. This will help you focus in on your best business connections and resources. It may be a good idea to see a career counselor or success coach to help you move from square one to square two, or to break down your job search into smaller, more realistic steps. If you are overwhelmed, you will block your intuitive messages.

Some people are so deathly afraid of putting their ideas out there—so terrified of being plagiarized or imitated—that it cripples them. They end up never risking anything.

The two of us have had more bad copycats than Elvis. We've actually had our identity as the Psychic Twins stolen by two people who weren't even twins! While this was annoying, to say the least, we just kept moving ahead. We were determined to become so well known that this kind of con would be impossible. You can't let your fears stop you. It can be death to the intuitive spirit.

You can do the market research, hold focus groups, and consult the experts, but in the end you need to "go with your gut" and trust that what your intuition is telling you is correct.

Tune In to Your Kids

If your child is using drugs and lying about it, your intuition will help you notice the telltale signs and bring key issues to the surface. Or, is your child involved with an abuser? Many kids won't tell anyone if they are, especially if they have been threatened. Your Clairs will keep you tuned in to the clues—dropping grades, personality changes, unusual or inexplicable mood swings, avoidance of communication—so that you'll notice and intercede before it's too late.

As we were writing this, the headlines were full of tragic stories about kids who had been bullied by their peers to the point where they committed suicide. In almost all these cases the victims' parents said afterward that they "had no idea" what was going on. Why? Because teenagers often bottle up their feelings or are too afraid to talk to their parents, especially if they feel that they are in some way guilty of having provoked the bullying behavior. But how did all these parents miss the warning signs that were surely there? Sure, they were probably working, stressed out, and overextended to the max, but the problem goes deeper than that. It has to do with being plugged in to your kids through your Clairs. Getting in touch with your psychic intelligence can clue you in to your child's secret thoughts, actions, needs, desires, and fears. You have it within your power to possibly prevent a tragedy waiting to happen.

IS THIS PSYCHIC SENSE OR COMMON SENSE?—TAKE THE QUIZ!

Some of what we've been talking about probably does sound to you a lot like using your common sense. Psychic sense and common sense overlap, but psychic sense actually goes beyond common sense. So if you think something sounds like common sense, it may be because you're more psychic than you think.

Circle P or C for each of the following statements:

1. You don't let your six-year-old play out in the yard unsupervised.   P C
2. You don't let your new guy friend babysit while you get a manicure.   P C
3. You suddenly have a bad feeling about a guy you're dating.   P C
4. You avoid eating peanuts because you are allergic.   P C
5. You don't eat the tuna surprise on a cruise ship, because you get a funny feeling.   P C
6. You want to buy a house, but you don't because you just lost your job.   P C
7. You say no when your gay friend asks you to marry him so he can get a green card.   P C
8. Something tells you your teenager is lying, even though you don't know why. You search his closet and find drug paraphernalia.   P C
9. Your new boyfriend disappears for days at a time, and you decide to dump him.   P C

(*Continued*)

10. You get an urge to turn down a street, and when you do, you see that the house you've been visualizing for years is for sale.   P   C

11. You find a lump under your arm and schedule a doctor's appointment to check it out.   P   C

12. You have a dream that your friend has an illness, and you share the dream with her.   P   C

13. You don't go jogging alone on a deserted road at night.   P   C

14. You want to take the boat out but a storm is brewing, so you don't go.   P   C

15. You know exactly how much your car repair bill will be before it arrives.   P   C

16. You decide to go to a business convention because you have a feeling you'll meet a guy there who has the start-up capital you need for your franchise.   P   C

17. You see an ad for what sounds like your dream job, but you know the address and it's in a residential neighborhood, not the business district, so you don't pursue it.   P   C

18. You have a bad dream and decide to postpone a flight out of town. The next day you learn that there has been a hijacking threat at the same airport.   P   C

19. You have the idea to Google an old friend from high school and wind up dating him.   P   C

Answer Key:
Psychic: 3, 5, 8, 10, 15, 16, 18, 19
Common Sense: 1, 2, 4, 6, 7, 9, 11, 12, 13, 14, 17

One of the times when using our psychic intelligence can help us the most is also the time when most people tend to ignore it—and that's when we're in love, think we're in love, or when we're looking for someone to share our life. In the next chapter you'll learn all about how to use your intuition to enhance romance and avoid potentially toxic partners.

18

Use Psychic Intelligence to Find Love and Marriage

Love may be blind, but using your inner vision is one way to ensure that you won't be blindsided. Don't get sidetracked by Mr. or Ms. Wrong and waste your time or risk real emotional—or even physical—pain and suffering.

Trust Your Dating Vibes

The trouble with being psychic is that every time you go on a date you may wind up psychically previewing the potential divorce and ensuing custody battle. There's no spoiler alert to warn you that the outcome is about to be revealed.

Years ago, Terry was dating a guy named Scott. He was successful, tall, handsome, and athletic, but Terry had a bad feeling about him. He seemed too aggressive and when she broke up with him, he was extremely angry—almost violent. She knew she had dodged a bullet when she later found out that Scott had since married and was physically abusive to his wife. Developing and trusting your psychic intelligence can protect you from that kind of abuse.

THE LOVE QUIZ—WHAT'S YOUR ROMANCE QUOTIENT?

To find your paranormal paramour, you need to start channeling your inner cupid! First, get to know yourself and recognize your patterns. You can't change what you don't acknowledge.

Circle as many of the following answers as you feel apply to you:

1. Which TV show best applies to your current relationship?
   a) *Family Guy*
   b) *Desperate Housewives*
   c) *The Odd Couple*
   d) *Three's Company*
   e) *Mad About You*
   f) *Mission: Impossible*
2. Which game show best describes your dating history?
   a) *Wheel of Fortune*
   b) *Deal or No Deal*
   c) *Who Wants to Be a Millionaire*
   d) *The Price Is Right*
   e) *The Dating Game*
   f) *Jeopardy!*
3. Which reality show best describes your life?
   a) *Jersey Shore*
   b) *Fear Factor*
   c) *The Biggest Loser*
   d) *Punk'd*
   e) *RuPaul's Drag Race*
   f) *The Surreal Life*
4. Which movie or TV show best describes you?
   a) *The Devil Wears Prada*
   b) *Wonder Woman*
   c) *Unsolved Mysteries*

d) *Clueless*

e) *Mommie Dearest*

f) *Dumb and Dumber*

5. Which TV show best describes the type of person you usually attract?

a) *Monday Night Football*

b) *Freaks and Geeks*

c) *Married... With Children*

d) *The Bachelor*

e) *The Bionic Woman*

f) *Gimme a Break!*

We hope that taking this quiz has not only given you a good laugh but also helped you to recognize a pattern in the way you've been conducting your dating life.

Be Your Own Love Psychic

Let's face it, we are all looking for love, that special person who completes us. But if you use your wits—and the four Clairs—you'll do a lot better with a lot less stress!

We met Kate at our friend's birthday party. Her eyes lit up when we told her we were psychics, and she confided that she, too, was very intuitive. Then she told us the story of meeting her husband, Ben, twenty years earlier. She had been living in Maryland and had fallen in love with a man we'll call "Kevin." They were planning to move to Seattle together, but Kate got there ahead of Kevin and, on the very first day, met Ben, a man who lived in her new apartment building. In a very short time Kate realized that she was falling in love with Ben, and after meditating on the situation she realized that she would have to end her engagement to Kevin, who was, understandably, heartbroken. Many years later, still happily married to Ben, Kate decided to Google her one-time love and was shocked to learn that he had died in a car accident. We believe that an angel put Ben in Kate's path. But she then needed to listen to her own inner voice and follow her heart in order to make the best choice for herself. Because she was already engaged to Kevin, she could have shut down her feelings for Ben and refused to even consider that she had another option, but she didn't do that. She allowed her intuition to lead her to true love and a better life.

In another story of finding true love, our friend Lexie had gone on dozens of dates with successful men who wined and dined her. Many of these men proposed, but it never felt "right." When Lexie came to us for advice, we encouraged her to continue dating. But when she insisted that she was going to be married within one year, come hell or high water, we felt that her energy was desperate and cautioned that it would actually be three years, and that she would meet her future husband through a personal ad. She argued with us, insisting that she would prove us wrong. Our timeframe simply didn't fit her plan.

In spite of her resistance, we soldiered on and gave her some advice about how to attract the right guy. We told her that she'd be surprised because he wouldn't fit the picture she had in her head, and we suggested that she try dating guys who were a bit more secure and a bit less flashy. "Be more flexible," we said. "And don't rush into a physical relationship. Try getting to know the men you date on a deeper level, and meet their family and friends." We also encouraged her to meditate every day, to cut back on her alcohol use, and to make a list of the top ten nonnegotiable characteristics she required in a partner.

As a result of our counseling, Lexie felt guided to join a couple of dating websites and started to be more open-minded about the guys she was considering as potential partners. She moved out of the city to a suburb where the lifestyle was more relaxed, and she began meditating on her own every morning, visualizing the type of man she wanted to be with. Sure enough, three years later to the month, she met Adam, a successful film producer, through the personals. She invited us both to her dream wedding, and they have been happily married for eight years now.

And here's a third true-love story. Tanya, a writer, told us that she had predicted, six months in advance, the exact date when she would meet her soul mate. When she and Matthew met behind the scenes at a concert, it was a real love-at-first-sight experience. She literally saw him surrounded by a golden aura of light, and from the first moment they both knew that they would always be together. Tanya's natural clairvoyance and claircognizance showed her that this guy was the right one, and she trusted her psychic intelligence.

But love at first sight doesn't necessarily mean you're clairvoyant. It could also mean that the object of your affection happens to fit your mental image or expectation. You may be fooling yourself and wind up missing out on the real Mr. or Ms. Right just because he or she doesn't fit your picture.

We knew a man of seventy who was only attracted to women in their twenties. We were shocked when Bill said he was considering calling Britney Spears up for a date! "On a scale from one to ten you are looking for a ten. But are *you* a ten, Bill?" Terry asked him. He was completely stymied by that question! Clearly, he viewed himself as perfect and ruled out anyone who might be even slightly available. This was his way of protecting himself from a real relationship. Bill would go to dances, where he was approached by many attractive women who were over forty and fifty, but they were never good enough. He was fixated on the unattainable ideal woman, the celebrity in a glossy magazine whom he would never likely meet.

When you're on a date, listen with your inner ear. Do you share this person's goals and values? What do they say about their ex-partners? Are you hearing more than you ever wanted to about this person's divorce? Do they listen to you or just talk? In a restaurant, notice the language they use, and what they say to the waitstaff. We can pick up on a lot of character clues in one conversation. Go back to the previous chapter and reread the section on how to become a better judge of character.

When you're with the right person, you should be happy and relaxed. You should feel positive energy flowing between you. If you feel awkward, anxious, or drained, don't dismiss those feelings. Do you feel as if your shoulders are hunched up around your neck? If your body is tense and giving you negative feedback, pay attention. Trust the vibes you get. Don't confuse lust with love. If you drink too much, you won't be as aware of your true feelings, so try to limit yourself to one or two drinks.

The two of us can usually predict down to the nanosecond how long we will date someone. (Terry finds this particularly annoying because Linda will say, "You're going to date him for two weeks and ten minutes." And she'll always be right.) That is because we use all four of our Clairs! When you're with someone, notice what thoughts are running through your mind: Is he or she truthful? Interested? Sincere? Respectful? Does he or she give you only a cell phone number? Is this person unavailable on holidays? Does he or she seem too smooth or too nervous around you? Is he secretive about how he spends his free time?

AFFIRMATIONS FOR FINDING TRUE LOVE

- I am willing to risk opening up to love.
- I surrender to love now.
- I attract powerful, loving relationships.
- I deserve love.
- The right person comes into my life for my happiness.
- I acknowledge the gifts and lessons of my past relationships.
- I release old beliefs about love.
- I am ready to attract my soul mate.
- I reach out to connect my heart with the heart of my true love.
- I easily attract love into my life.
- I am willing to take action to meet the right person.
- I am committed to a breakthrough in my love life now.
- I am loving and lovable.

Psychic Love—Attract Your True Mate

Many of us tend to worship at the "Shrine of the Holy Soul Mate." When we are lost in love, most of us can miss even the most glaring warning signs in a romantic partnership. The initial period of romantic desire when we can be carried away by unreasoned passion is called "limerance," a term coined by a psychologist to describe the obsessive infatuation of falling in love. True feelings of love can take months or even years to develop. To avoid unnecessary dating distress, follow your Clairs!

We so often see people, both male and female, making disastrous marriage decisions and ending up in divorce court. Many women, for example, inherit debt that they had no idea their husband had before the marriage. Shortly after New Year's 1998, Linda had a premonition that she would meet a man on March fifth. Amazingly, on that very day a friend introduced her to Taylor, an acupuncturist and naturopath, and they began dating. Taylor built Linda a few pieces of furniture, which made a good first impression. For a while she felt adored and cherished. He gave her back massages and made her feel special. He even indicated that he was financially stable and ready to buy a house and settle down with the right person. They had been dating a few months when one night, out of nowhere, Terry said, "He has sixty thousand dollars in debt that he hasn't told you about." Sure enough, Linda found out that very night that Terry was correct, down to the dollar, when Taylor sheepishly confessed it without any prompting. It was hard to walk away from a guy who built coffee tables and had a healing gift, but Linda knew that having so much debt was a deal-breaker. They broke up a short time later.

We hear and read every day about people who were blindsided by a spouse's infidelity or some financial indiscretion because they were so focused on the fantasy of the life they'd imagined that they failed to tune in to the reality of the actual situation. In his bestselling biography *Diana: Her True Story in Her Own Words*, Andrew Morton quotes the late princess Diana as saying, "The night before the wedding I was very, very calm, deathly calm. I felt I was a lamb to the slaughter. I knew it and couldn't do anything about it." Unfortunately, she got the feeling too late, and the rest is history. We suspect that if she had tuned in to her psychic intelligence sooner, she might well have avoided a great deal of heartbreak down the road.

MARIANNA'S STORY

Marianna, a young woman in her late thirties, called us for a phone reading. Her husband, Ryan, had left her and their two young children for another woman, someone they both worked with. We correctly intuited that he had recently started drinking again. Now, he was coming around a lot, wanting to spend more time with Marianna.

Despite being close to forty in chronological age, this guy was still a teenager emotionally. He was absolutely terrified of intimacy and allergic to commitment. Having a baby had proved to be too much work and responsibility for him. We explained to Marianna that if there were to be any hope of their marriage succeeding, they would have to get into some serious marriage counseling. Meanwhile, we also picked up the strong sense that Ryan was still seeing the other woman. Marianna was levelheaded and intelligent, but her role had become that of a parent with Ryan.

We asked Marianna if her husband had a difficult home life growing up, and she admitted he had. His mother had left, and his father had been abusive. We perceived that his attitude was, "I'll leave you before you leave me." We also told her that we didn't see him staying with his current mistress long; he would leave as soon as it looked like he might have to make a commitment. Deep down, Ryan wanted to remain a bachelor, without any hassle or responsibilities of any kind.

Marianna just wanted Ryan to tell her what was wrong—that is, what was wrong with *her*. "That's just it," we told her. "You're not wrong here. These are his personal issues, and he has to decide to work on himself. He doesn't seem to care how much pain he's caused you.

And you need to realize how great you are. You really deserve better."
Marianna had to agree there!

In this case, we accurately predicted the following information, and
Marianna confirmed it:

- Ryan was still cheating on her and lying about it.
- He refused to go to counseling.
- He was drinking and smoking pot, which clouded his judgment.
  We got this information psychically, but she corroborated it.
- He was unwilling to change his behavior.

"You could stay with Ryan, but he won't stop cheating on you," we
said. "The choice is yours." In this case, the price is not worth the payoff, we cautioned her. In trying to make him into the "perfect husband,"
she had overlooked all the negatives. We then predicted a future long-
term partner we saw for her if she were able to leave Ryan, and we
described him in detail. When we hung up, Marianna promised to meditate on everything we had told her, and thanked us for our insights.
These days, Marianna reports that she is happily living on her own and
raising her children.

If you get a sense that your partner or fiancé is not being totally
honest or is withholding information, pay attention to those feelings.
Your psychic intelligence will help you discern if this person is truthful
and can be depended upon in the years to come, before you get in over
your head. Some of the following questions may seem too extreme to
even consider, but many people who have brushed them aside have
later lived to regret not paying more attention to the psychic signs.

- What is their financial track record?
- Do they have a heavy load of debt for which you might become
  responsible?
- Have they been financially dependent on prior partners?

- Are their long-term (financial or family) goals and values compatible with yours?
- Do they *really* seem to enjoy the same things you do, or do you get the feeling that they're just pretending in order to make you happy?
- Have you met their family? How do they treat them? Do they speak of family with love and respect?
- Have you met their friends? Are they people whose company you enjoy?
- What do your friends think of the person you're dating?
- Do you trust that they have your best interests at heart?
- What is their dating track record?
- Have they been divorced? If so, do you know why the marriage ended?
- She says she is using birth control, but is she trying to trap you with a pregnancy?
- He tells you he wants children, but is he just playing you?

Sometimes when things seem too good, that also can be a warning sign. Remember that sociopaths are often great charmers. No one is perfect, so if the person you're dating doesn't seem to have a single flaw, our advice is to watch out! Get those psychic antennae up and be on the alert for danger signals.

THE DANGER OF SELF-DELUSION: KRISTEN'S STORY

A young woman we'll call "Kristen" scheduled a phone reading with us because she was anxious to know the future of her marriage. Before she called, the two of us prepared as always with meditation and chanting. When we used our automatic writing to tune in to her current state of affairs, it became immediately clear that there was a lot of trouble in paradise. We saw that her husband, whom we'll call "Daniel," was angry, controlling, and there was abuse on both sides.

Kristen was extremely anxious and did not admit the truth right away. We were amazed at how many times she was able to delude herself about the reality of the situation.

Terry told her, "It is important for you to trust your inner guidance and admit the truth, Kristen. Your husband has not been faithful to you. You are very fiery together, and he has been physically and emotionally abusive. Is this true?" At first Kristen denied it, insisting that her husband was a "good person." But after about thirty minutes, she finally admitted that they had been separated for eight months after much fighting, and a lot of abuse on both their parts. We advised her that going for marriage counseling was the only way they could make the marriage work.

Kristen, however, wanted an instant fix and a guarantee that she could make her marriage work. We told her that no one could give her an insurance policy and that working through her issues with Daniel in therapy would be the only possible way to save their marriage. She then confessed that they had tried therapy briefly, but nothing had changed.

Kristen was unwilling to see her husband for who he really was. "He pushes you away with his anger because he fears intimacy," Terry said. We spoke to her about his family, too, and it turned out that we were right. Daniel's family had completely judged and rejected Kristen from the beginning, and she had ignored all the warning signs that were there even before their wedding.

"It is so important that you take back your own power, Kristen," Linda told her. "You need to meditate and build your faith and spiritual wealth—develop your character with what you are learning here. You are not wasting your time." Linda counseled her not to compare herself with her friends who had successful marriages and children. "Your mission and life path are different from theirs," Linda said.

"If you just cut and run, you will end up attracting the same kind of guy who is not right for you," Terry added. "There is no perfect man or perfect marriage. It will just be 'same music, different partner.' When we marry, we marry the man and his entire family. You are in a difficult

(Continued)

situation here. Physical abuse is a deal-breaker. We are not saying you can't make this work, but you both must want to commit one hundred percent to counseling and learning a new way of communicating."

Linda also told Kristen that she needed to learn how to listen. As we were talking with her, we could barely get a sentence out before she interrupted with a new question. We told her that by practicing the art of listening to others, she would open up to hearing the deeper voice of her intuition as well. We told her to love and trust herself. When we said good-bye, Kristen told us that she was extremely grateful for the help!

She later told us that she had filed for divorce from Daniel. She said she was much happier, casually dating several different men, and enjoying her life. She was no longer focused on finding her identity through a man, and she had enrolled in community college.

Keep Your Mind and Heart Open

We've been telling you about paying attention to the warning signs your Clairs are sending, but there is also the potential danger that you will close yourself off from any romantic possibilities. Ultimately, using your psychic intelligence is all about keeping an open mind.

Are you someone who constantly complains that "all men are jerks" or "there are no good women to date"? We had a friend like that. No one was ever good enough for Cindy. She had been betrayed more than once because she had a pattern of attracting men who were emotionally unavailable, and, as a result, she'd cut herself off completely from the possibility of finding a mate. We told her that her perceptions were not accurate and that her belief that men were all the same was just that—a belief. "You complain all the time about what's wrong with men, yet many women are happy in their relationships," we told her. "You are making poor choices because you are afraid of getting hurt again." Cindy was speechless. No one had ever been this honest with her, and it had never occurred to her that she might be wrong. Once she recognized that her negativity was attracting negative men, Cindy was able to change her expectations. As she shifted her beliefs about men, she started to approach dating with a more open mind. It took awhile, but Cindy eventually met a guy with whom she is very compatible, and she is learning to be more trusting and accepting.

Not so long ago, we met three wonderfully funny Eastern European women in their sixties who were only too willing to give us their opinions about love and marriage. "When you are married," one of them said, "you have a *million* problems. When you are single, only one: you're not married!" Then another of them chimed in, stating unequivocally, "I will *never* get married again. Not even if he is *rich*!" She sliced the air dramatically with her hands to punctuate her comments. We all had to laugh. Negativity is one sure way to cut yourself off from romance, but another is having too many unrealistic expectations.

You can pass the right person by because of some "must" or "must not" rule you've set in place in advance. Having those rules can get in the way of your paying attention to your Clairs. You might, for example, be intuitively drawn to someone who doesn't quite fit the mental picture you've already painted of your perfect mate and, therefore, ignore what your psychic intelligence is trying to tell you. It's really not so different from refusing to listen to good advice because you just don't want to hear it. Do you have preconceived notions about Mr. or Ms. Right such as:

- He must be a perfect dancer.
- He must be over six feet tall.
- He must be older/younger than I am.
- She must be blond.
- She must love baseball.
- She must bake lasagna like my mother.
- He must earn a six-figure income.
- He must not have a pet.

- She must not want a career outside the home.
- She must not make more money than I do.

If so, ask yourself why those particular attributes should be deal-breakers for you. You may find that they're not so important after all.

It's All about Balance

Having more insight into our own patterns and behaviors opens up our intuition, and that naturally builds our self-confidence. If we want a healthy partner, we must become a healthy and balanced person first. Don't look so hard for someone else to complete you. As you develop your four Clairs, you will naturally cultivate your wisdom and magnetism. Awareness, confidence, and action are the secret ingredients for attracting the love you desire.

At the end of the day, to attract true love we need to truly love ourselves. And to do that, we first need to know who we are. We need to figure out who we are at the core, when we're being our most authentic self. In the next chapter, we'll be helping you to make that all-important discovery.

19

Become Your Most Authentic Self

Who do you think you are? Most people equate who they are with what they do—I'm a doctor, a ballet dancer, a computer tech, a mom—but your occupation is only one small aspect of your identity. Your true identity is your authentic self, composed of every aspect of your being, from your passions to your emotions to your joys and sorrows, your greatest accomplishments and, yes, your biggest failures. Using your psychic intelligence is the best way we know to find that authentic core within yourself and allow it to flourish. We believe that every single one of us owes it to ourself to do that.

When we lose touch with our authentic self, we may try to fill that void with food, sex, or alcohol, or we may lose ourselves in our work. It is important to discover whose life it is anyway. You alone can answer that question, and you may pay a heavy price if you don't.

The Japanese word for mission is *"shimei,"* which means "to use one's life."

Having a clear sense of your true purpose gives you passion and focus. What brings your life meaning? Too many of us never ask ourselves this question, yet it is the most important question we can ask.

THE DIFFERENCE BETWEEN RELATIVE AND ABSOLUTE HAPPINESS

In Buddhism, there are two kinds of happiness: relative and absolute. Buddhist leader and educator Daisaku Ikeda defines the difference this way:

> Relative happiness is happiness that depends on things outside ourselves: friends, and family, surroundings, the size of our home or family income. This is what we feel when a desire is fulfilled, or something we have longed for is obtained. While the happiness such things bring us is certainly real, the fact is that none of this lasts forever. Things change. People change. This kind of happiness shatters easily when external conditions are altered.
>
> Relative happiness is also based on comparison with others. We may feel this kind of happiness when we get a newer or bigger home than the neighbors. But that feeling turns to misery the moment they start making new additions to theirs!
>
> Absolute happiness, on the other hand, is something we must find within. It means establishing a state of life in which we are never defeated by trials and where just being alive is a source of great joy. This persists no matter what we might be lacking, or what might happen around us. A deep sense of joy is something that can exist only in the innermost reaches of our life, and that cannot be destroyed by any external forces. It's eternal and inexhaustible.

Absolute happiness resides deep within ourselves, and that is where we need to look for it. It is the purpose for which our soul was put on this earth—our higher purpose, if you will. And the way to find it is to use our higher intelligence. Ask yourself: "What really inspires me? What winds my clock or floats my boat? What brings a smile to my face when I think about doing it?" Make a daily effort to connect with your inner psychic self through meditation, yoga, or simply a walk in nature. Allow the ideas to germinate and gently rise to the surface of your consciousness. It may take some time, but you'll find that, day by day, you are gaining a sense of clarity, and feeling more centered. Once you discover your higher purpose, you will find that it is easier to find meaning and a sense of hope in your personal life—even when it seems hopeless.

What is meaningful to you? Your children? Your friends? Taking care of a parent? Do you volunteer? Do you contribute to your community? Who is meaningful in your life? How do you want to use *your* life?

What Would You Like to Do Over?

Most of us start out with some dream for our future, but very often that dream gets lost or buried or tossed by the wayside. As the years go by, we take on more and more responsibilities and, before we know it, we get stuck in a rut. We have lost not only our dreams but also ourselves. One way to start recapturing those lost dreams is to try to recall the person we were all those years ago. To help you do that, complete the following sentences with the first thought that comes into your mind: Don't overthink it; the idea is to let your gut feelings dictate your responses.

- As a child I felt:
  a) like an alien
  b) loved
  c) lonely
  d) awkward
  e) insecure
  f) confident
  g) shy
- When I was a child, my favorite hobby was _____.
- As a child, I wish I could have done more _____.

- I wanted to be _____ when I grew up.
- My first intuitive experience was _____.
- My best friend was _____.
- My favorite place to travel was _____.
- My relationship with my mother was _____.
- My relationship with my father was _____.
- My favorite teacher was _____.
- My favorite television show was _____.
- My feelings about death were _____.
- The most important lesson I learned about money was _____.
- The most important lesson I learned about life was _____.
- My favorite game was _____.
- My favorite sport was _____.
- I used to dream a lot about _____.
- My favorite memory about elementary school is _____.
- My favorite memory about high school is _____.
- I am proudest of _____.
- My favorite pet was _____.
- I always held myself back from _____.
- My childhood hero was _____.
- My favorite music or band was _____.
- One bridge I regret burning is _____.

Now think about how your answers relate to your life today. You may still be enjoying the same things, or there may be activities you've given up that you'd like to pursue again. Perhaps you had a goal that you still dream of accomplishing. Sometimes we follow a certain path and never look back. We try not to think about the road not taken. Now is the time to think about it and consider whether you'd like to retrace your steps and take a different route, maybe even move to a different place. It's never too late to start over if that's what you truly want. And sometimes taking a look over your shoulder and seeing where you've been is just what it takes to reconsider where you really want to go from here.

Rediscover Your Passion

As kids we tend to be passionate about everything. We *hate* broccoli. We *love* the color pink. We *can't stand* Brian, but we *adore* Rocco. There's almost nothing we feel wishy-washy about. But, again, with time, we seem to lose that passion. Instead of living a life filled with highs and lows, we actually prefer the middle road. The two of us have always believed that the middle road may be safe, but it's as boring as grits at an all-you-can-eat buffet. And if you don't take a chance, step outside the box, and follow your passion, your life will be passing by without your ever having fully lived.

In *Women's Bodies, Women's Wisdom,* Dr. Christiane Northrup writes, "When we can clearly state what we want and why, we are instantly in alignment with our inner guidance. This is because it feels good in our bodies to think about and dwell upon what we want and why. We get excited and are inspired automatically by these thoughts and feelings, which in turn keep us in touch with our inner knowing and spiritual energy. The result is enthusiasm and joy. Our culture has too often taught us that it is selfish to have our own wants and dreams and to enjoy ourselves." We agree with everything Dr. Northrup says, and we couldn't have put it any more beautifully or clearly ourselves. It's sad that so many of us feel selfish because we are doing what we love, or putting ourselves at the top of our to-do list. We must value our own lives, talents, and gifts as much as we value those of others. We must make ourselves our own first priority. That is using our psychic intelligence to understand why we are here.

JOURNALING EXERCISE—AN EXERCISE IN SELF-DISCOVERY

To get the most out of your life, you need to know what you really, truly want. To help you find that out, get out your journal and ask yourself the following questions. While the questions themselves sound simple and straightforward, we've found that many people never bother to ask them, or, if they do, they're at a loss to know how to answer them. Don't be too glib or quick in your responses here. Take the time to really think about each one so that your answers are as genuine as possible.

1. What do I love?
2. What places do I want to visit?
3. What hobby have I been postponing?
4. Whom would I most like to meet?
5. What are my favorite books?
6. Where do I feel most at home?
7. With whom do I want to reconnect?
8. If I don't express my passion, what will I regret the most at the end of my life?
9. If I could do anything, what would it be?
10. What is my number one goal in life? (To love, teach, be a parent, be the first woman president, win an Oscar, own a business?)
11. Am I willing to give myself the time to develop my true self?
12. Am I willing to pursue what I love, to discover my authentic self?
13. What are my strongest gifts, talents, and skills?
14. What are my greatest interests?
15. What activities make me truly happy?
16. Do I have unhealthy habits or addictions?
17. What is eating me, literally?

Now, don't just put your list away and forget about it. Use it as a starting point to do something new.

Write Your Own Bucket List

Have you seen the movie in which Jack Nicholson and Morgan Freeman set out on a road trip to do everything on their wish list before they die? If you had such a wish list, what would be on it? Here are a few suggestions to help you get started:

- I want to laugh till I cry.
- I want to conquer my fear of public speaking.
- I want to be a showgirl.
- I want to travel to Ireland.
- I want to finish my book.
- I want to reconnect with my father.
- I want to [fill in the blank].

Reinvent Yourself

It's never too late. People reinvent themselves all the time. We have had numerous careers and odd jobs, all of which led us to our current life path. We feel fortunate to have fulfilled some of our biggest dreams, even those we thought were impossible: becoming comedians, starring in films, and writing books were just a few of them. One woman we saw profiled on television had been a hard-driving businesswoman all her life, but she left her career to pursue her passion for knitting. She was so in love with knitting that she knit while walking and while waiting in bank lines. Her book on knitting sold 65,000 copies!

It's easy to underestimate other people's passions. For a long time (several decades, actually) our father didn't understand our obsession with psychic work and prediction, but now that he sees we are happy and successful, he is very supportive of what we do.

But finding your authentic self and life purpose is not really about accomplishment; it's about discovering the passion that is in your heart. As author Wayne Dyer says, "Don't die with your music still inside you. Listen to your intuitive inner voice and find what passion stirs your soul."

Sansho Shima or "The Devil You Say!"

TEN PSYCHIC TWINSIGHTS

1. What is true for you is true, whether or not it's true for anyone else.
2. To achieve peace you must embrace your sixth sense.
3. Go from magical thinking to magical *being*!
4. The Universe wants you to succeed.
5. Whatever you do affects countless others.
6. You are a part of a purpose greater than you realize.
7. Your soul has lived before and is here to fulfill a purpose.
8. Honor your unique perception of the world.
9. No one but you can define your mission.
10. Come from your heart and attract everything you need.

Sansho shima means "three obstacles and four devils" in Japanese. It refers specifically to the various types of difficulties people encounter when practicing Buddhism—particularly those that undermine their faith and prevent them from practicing. It can, however, be equally applied to any difficult or controversial endeavor, including the development of our psychic intelligence.

As a general rule, the more we evolve spiritually, the bigger the obstacles become. Buddhism teaches that "the fire gets hotter." We have within our lives what are called "devilish functions," and as we advance, these hindrances arise to try to stop us from achieving our goal. We noticed this when we first started chanting, and it has continued throughout our practice. But our lives are much stronger now, and we can navigate the rapids with more grace and courage than we ever could before. Our psychic intelligence has given us more flexibility in dealing with adversity, and we realize that we are much stronger than our difficulties.

What's important is our attitude toward these obstacles when they appear—because they will, whether we practice Buddhism or not. There will be ups and downs in our journey—that much is assured. We must learn to view these obstacles as opportunities to challenge ourselves through faith, and ultimately change our destiny.

At one point as we were writing this book, an interview with us was published in a magazine; we were writing our monthly newsletter and column; and we were in meetings with a TV production company. Then, right in the middle of all this productivity, our toilets and kitchen drains clogged, our computer crashed, our electrical switches went kerflooey, and both phone batteries died at the same time! We had so many computer guys and plumbers in and out that we were beginning to feel like the Marx Brothers in *Duck Soup*. To add insult to injury, on Easter Sunday we experienced a 7.2 earthquake in California! Yes, we had predicted it, but it's one thing to predict an earthquake and a whole different thing to actually live through one!

When life feels out of control like this we usually double up on our chanting and strengthen our determination that "all devils be crushed." And when we remember that everything always works out in the end, everything usually does. If you approach obstacles or crises with curiosity and optimism instead of panic, you'll find that problems become an interesting adventure.

When we were much younger and constantly struggling with serious health and financial problems at the same time we were trying to launch our careers, we embraced the Buddhist attitude "Never give up—no matter what," and as a surprising side benefit, our psychic abilities were greatly enhanced.

We believe that out of suffering will come your greatest gifts and blessings. The Buddhist saying *"Hendoku iyaku"* means "Turn poison to medicine." Whenever we had a bad experience, our Buddhist leaders exclaimed, "Congratulations!" With this frame of mind, every obstacle becomes an opportunity to prove the power each one of us has to overcome our own negativity.

We tell our students to "go past the thought." If you have a goal, and you have doubts about achieving it, press past the thought that you can't achieve it. "Take your head off" and do not strategize too much. If you want to act in a Hollywood movie, a million excuses for not being able to do that may come into your mind: "I live too far away; I never studied; I'm too old; I may be rejected. . . ." Go past the thought and open up to the possibility that other, more powerful, mystical forces will come into play. When you do that, your psychic intelligence will kick into gear and your spirit guides will assist you in finding a way for you to fulfill your dream.

People are hardwired to focus on the negative, the worst-case scenario. Because our thoughts have energy, we attract more of what we focus on, either consciously or subconsciously. The more positive our thoughts, the more positive things, people, and experiences we will draw into our orbit. Positive thinking isn't always enough to attract what we want, however. We may have subconscious, sabotaging beliefs that need to be dealt with. That is why a spiritual practice such as prayer, chanting, or meditation can be helpful. We encourage you to use positive self-statements like, "Things always work out for me"; "I thank the Universe for this _____ that I have already received"; "Even though this seems impossible, I can achieve what I want. I can make this happen."

Personally, we prefer to be optimists who are occasionally wrong rather than pessimists who insist on being right about there being no magic in the world.

To help increase your own optimism, try repeating to yourself:

I know that I am already on the mountaintop. I feel empowered. I can do anything I want. I am perfect and whole; I can push any button and shift my perceptions by reframing, using positive words. I choose to focus on reclaiming the power and perfection and health and wealth that are

already mine. It is easy to succeed and accomplish my goals
and dreams. I take my power back now. I am in charge of my
life, I am my own authority. In giving freely of my talents
and gifts, I uplift, encourage, and inspire others to be and
do better. The past doesn't count, and I no longer allow it to
influence me. I trust the divine timing.

Don't Be Psychic Stupid

Being "psychic stupid" is the term we've coined to describe those
times when we don't follow our inner voice, vision, or feeling. It is the
opposite of using your psychic intelligence. Terry admits that mar-
rying her first boyfriend at the age of twenty-two was "the dumbest
thing I ever did." In all fairness, she was not as in touch with her psychic abilities at that young age as she is now, but there were lots of red
flags on the field. And in any case, most of us don't have a clue about
who we are at that age, much less about whom we want to spend the
rest of our life with.

But being psychic stupid isn't necessarily a function of age. It happens any time you ignore your inner voice or guidance—when someone gives you good advice and you don't take it (or you take advice you
shouldn't), or when your gut is telling you something and you choose
to ignore it. Being psychic stupid can lead you to take the wrong job,
stay in a situation you shouldn't, invest your money badly, place your
trust foolishly—in effect, it impacts every single aspect of your life.

When you lose track of your psychic guidance system, you will
lose your way in life. You'll make bad decisions. You'll ignore all the
warning signs. You'll marry the wrong guy, or commit too soon.
You'll buy the wrong house. You'll get pregnant too young. You'll
substitute someone else's dream for your own.

Being psychic is about paying attention. When you really pay
close attention to details, you will unravel life's mysteries. Think of
your Clairs as seeds that you plant and nurture and help grow. That
being said, it is important to understand that this is about the journey,

not the end result. People are so focused on success these days that they often forget the importance of enjoying the experience of discovery and learning along the way. Compassion and heart matter more than being right.

It may take years to develop a true sense of who you are and learn to navigate the murky waters of the world. Keep tuning in; keep going deeper. Before making a decision ask yourself, "Does this decision feel right to me? Am I giving in and saying yes to this choice just to please someone else or gain his approval? Am I trying to prove something—and why? Is it risky for me? Am I giving in because everyone is doing it and I want to fit in? Will this make me happy? What's the downside?" It will help to list the pros and cons before tuning in with your psychic intelligence. Your intuition will guide you to the best decision for your life.

Avoid Magical Thinking

Magical thinking is not the same thing as tuning in to your psychic intelligence and using your Clairs. It is the mistaken belief that simply believing or thinking that something is possible is going to make it happen without any further effort on our part. When someone feels that wishing alone, devoid of action, will make something occur— that is magical thinking. We believe it is also a form of denial that prevents us from coping more positively with whatever problems we might have.

For example, we talk to people all the time who think they will become rich and famous just because they want it and dream about it. But prayer and wishing are not usually enough to manifest your dreams. Magical thinking is popular because, let's face it—who wants to work so hard to get somewhere? Our friend Lisa thought it was strange when we told her we actually keep people grounded in reality, because psychics are generally thought to be flaky or airy-fairy/ woo-woo types. Frankly, we don't think the airy-fairy approach will be much help to anyone. We don't let people get away with just hoping their lives will magically change without taking any concrete steps. But we do encourage them to take whatever steps they need to achieve what they truly want.

Be Unstoppable

You may have heard the old saying "The light at the end of the tunnel often turns out to be a train." As soon as you have a clear vision of your dream, get ready! We experienced a perpetual flood of people trying to rain on our parade. When you have a dream, there will be those who try to stop you, discourage you, trip you up, slow you down, get in your way, cramp your style, and kill your buzz. Don't let them, because if you do you might find yourself living someone else's dream, or missing out on your own.

We hope we have opened a doorway of understanding to the powers of your mind, and started you on a mystical journey. Using your psychic intelligence can enrich your life in myriad ways. Come to your senses—literally! You will discover a whole new realm of possibilities waiting for you.

Whenever you find yourself thinking that someone else can do something you can't, don't let fear get the best of you. Successful people take risks and don't give up on themselves, even when the going gets tough. As we've said, we had to deal with all kinds of illnesses and an army of doctors who gave up on us. We were often stretched to the max financially, and for many years, things were beyond bleak and verging on the ridiculous. Our family and friends didn't support our work. They were well intentioned, but we were completely on our own. In the end, it was our faith that saved us—and our connection to spirit. Against all odds, we managed to reach our goals because we challenged our own weaknesses on a daily basis. Don't let the critics get you down. The hardest part for us was that we truly had no role models in the psychic field to whom we could look for guidance. But we did have the invisible world of spirit, and our faith in that is what saved our lives.

We feel we are living very true to our heart and values, not in accordance with anyone's agenda but our own. We have always followed our inner compass, our deepest instincts, never conforming to anyone else's value system. It has been painful, difficult, and yes, we have paid the price for it. But the payoff is worth everything we've been through and more. We are free. No one rules us. We have never lost touch with what's sacred. We have what we need.

Pursue your dream and don't give your power away to others. Pursue it with a passion. No holding back. You and you alone know in your heart what your dream is. The path to psychic intelligence leads to wholeness and an expanded vision of what is possible in our lives. As we break free of old limiting patterns of thought, we can open up to new ways of being in the world. This is the path of true power.

Epilogue

We Are All One

The Spirit world is already here; all worlds interpenetrate each
other, nothing dies.

—Gordon Higginson, British medium

The way we go about our daily lives is based upon the assumption of separateness in terms of both time and space. We are separate from you; the table is separate from the chair; you are doing one thing while we are doing another. Our lives are sequential: First we do one thing, then another. If the second thing we do is in a different place from the first, we must leave enough time to get there. Even on an intellectual level science has shown that we can't hold two different thoughts simultaneously.

In truth, however, what we perceive to be the temporal and linear separation of all things is an illusion. The ego creates this sense that each of us is an individual, separate from everyone else. The illusion is a necessary construct for the maintenance of our sanity and to live in the world, but we need to remember that it is just that—an illusion.

The Connection beneath the Illusion

In ancient times the connection between our temporal lives on earth
and the eternal lives of ethereal beings was virtually taken for granted.
The gods who dwelt on Mount Olympus regularly came to earth to
affect the lives of men and then returned to their heavenly home. In
the fourth century BC Plato wrote that "this world is indeed a living
being endowed with a soul and intelligence ... a single visible living
entity containing all other living entities, which by their nature are
all related." In the Bible, prophets walked the earth to deliver God's
messages. And in the sixteenth century the Belgian philosopher and
alchemist Gerhard Dorn wrote about the *unus mundus*, that ultimate
realm of being "where splits are healed, duality ceases," and individuals are transformed back into the original, undivided unity of the
world soul.

In modern times, this concept of the world soul was described by
Swiss psychiatrist Carl Jung as the collective unconscious, "a second
psychic system of a collective, universal, and impersonal nature which
is identical in all individuals." Closely tied to this concept was Jung's
principle of synchronicity—the occurrence of concurrent events that
appear to be coincidental but that, when viewed from the perspective
of the collective unconscious, do have a causal relationship.

As psychics we strongly believe that there are no coincidences
and that whatever comes into our world is there for a reason. We
believe that we have each chosen to incarnate on this earth in order to
learn certain lessons, and dealing with challenges is going to help us
fulfill our own life purpose. The people and situations we encounter
on our life path are presenting us with opportunities to change and
evolve spiritually. They are our teachers and our mirrors, reflecting
back to us the beauty, strength, or weakness of our character. There
is a divine perfection to everything that happens. We may or may not
make the most of the opportunities we are given—because, as we've
said, we all have free will. But when we do take the opportunities
we are given to use our psychic intelligence and thereby discover our

most authentic selves, we will be contributing something to the Universe. That is how we fulfill our soul's purpose.

Confirmation from the World of Science

In 1972 MIT professor Edward Lorenz coined the term "butterfly effect" to exemplify the premise that a small and apparently inconsequential event (such as the flap of a butterfly's wings in Brazil) can have a significant and apparently unrelated effect elsewhere (such as a tornado in Texas). But experimental physicist John Bell had already demonstrated the truth of that theory on the subatomic level when, in the early 1960s, he performed an experiment showing that two particles continued to affect each other irrespective of the distance between them.

In quantum physics this effect is called "nonlocal causation." In everyday life, we assume that there must be some form of contact between two entities to create cause and effect (although in twenty-first-century terms, that contact could very well be electronic). What Bell's theorem proved, however, would be the equivalent of your swinging a tennis racquet in Arthur Ashe Stadium and thereby causing a ball to fly through the air at Wimbledon.

In January 2010, an article in *Coast to Coast AM*'s *After Dark* newsletter stated that "British physicist Brian Josephson, winner of the Nobel Prize, publicly stated in 2001 that there was a significant amount of evidence supporting the existence of telepathy (mind to mind communication). Scientific journals refused to publish his findings, claiming that it related to the paranormal and was therefore not scientific. Josephson stated that some people with psychic ability may be able to direct random energy on subatomic levels. He also believes that as quantum physics continues to develop, it may well reveal more about telepathy that science cannot account for."

What this means for every one of us is that everything we do, every decision we make, affects the Universe as a whole—even though we can't see or understand it at the time. It means that there is a reality beyond what we can see or touch every day and that, in terms of that larger reality, we are all connected to one another.

Bridging the Gap between Me and Us

So how do we bridge the gap between what is mundane reality and the cosmic ideal? As Deepak Chopra writes in his book *The Spontaneous Fulfillment of Desire,* "Real archetypes are enacted by people like Mahatma Gandhi, Martin Luther King Jr., Rosa Parks, anyone who reaches beyond daily life into the realm of the wondrous."

People achieve greatness because they are able to see beyond the immediate reality and understand how the choices they make in the present will affect not only their own future but the future of the planet. We believe this is what happens when we tap into our psychic abilities to change our own life, to help change the lives of others, and to make our predictions. We are accessing a level of knowing that exists beyond the temporal here-and-now and receiving information from a higher realm.

We are vibrational or energetic beings, all interconnected with one another by a vast ocean of molecules and atoms. Our spirits have no boundaries. On a cosmic level, our minds are part of a divine matrix—a unified mind, if you will. Spiritually, what connects us all is the vibration of love.

The Cosmic Love Connection

When we are able to recognize the ways we are all connected rather than the ways we are separated from one another, we are participating in a universal love connection. It is through these connections that we are able to experience what some call God and others might call the Higher Power, or the universal consciousness.

Linda has expressed her own concept of the universal love connection in a poem she calls "Precious."

Precious is jewel
Cosmic heart mind
The sacred ungraspable moment

Precious.
The language of tears and smiles
It can only be moments

The kind of love one receives only through
The gifting of love
And giving out of pure unattachment to receiving

Precious connection.

Infinite kindness, magic
The sharing of one's dearest thoughts
The generosity of a gesture, an outstretched hand,
A single word spoken to calm the fear.

Precious is our unique self
Expecting, open, joyful
Timeless, beyond knowing.

We believe that our purpose on this earth is to connect with others by being of service however and whenever we can. Most of us have an innate desire and capacity to love and contribute to the betterment of our world. Our good deeds are like stones thrown into a pond, sending endless ripples out in every direction. So, let us ask you:

- Are you a member of a community?
- What do you want to contribute to your community?
- What cause means the most to you?
- How can people from different backgrounds better appreciate and help one another?

- How have you contributed to the well-being of others?
- What small thing can you do today that will enrich another's life?

We urge you to ask the simple question "How can I be of service?" The answer will be given, that we promise.

As the Buddhist scripture says:

> Let your love flow outward through the universe,
> To its height, its depth, its broad extent,
> A limitless love, without hatred or enmity.
> Then as you stand or walk,
> Sit or lie down,
> As long as you are awake,
> Strive for this with a one-pointed mind;
> Your life will bring heaven to earth.
>
> —Sutta Nipata

We all must first heal ourselves so that we can then unite for healing the planet, because collectively we can each contribute to the creation of a healthier, happier world.

At the deepest level, we are all one.

> And may God bless you with enough foolishness to believe
> that you can make a difference in the world, so that you
> can do what others claim cannot be done.
>
> —Franciscan benediction